Business and Industry

EDITORS

William R. Childs
Scott B. Martin
Wanda Stitt-Gohdes

VOLUME 8

PRICE CONTROLS
to SARNOFF, DAVID

MARSHALL CAVENDISH
NEW YORK · TORONTO · LONDON · SYDNEY

Marshall Cavendish
99 White Plains Road
Tarrytown, New York 10591-9001

www.marshallcavendish.com

© 2004 Marshall Cavendish Corporation

Library of Congress Cataloging-in-Publication Data

Business and industry / editors, William R. Childs, Scott B. Martin, Wanda Stitt-Gohdes.
    p. cm.
  Includes bibliographical reference and index.
  Contents: v. 1. Accounting and Bookkeeping to Burnett, Leo--v. 2. Business Cycles to Copyright--
v. 3. Corporate Governance to Entrepreneurship--v. 4. Environmentalism to Graham,
Katharine--v. 5. Great Depression to Internship--v. 6. Inventory to Merrill Lynch--
v. 7. Microeconomics to Philip Morris Companies--v. 8. Price Controls to Sarnoff, David--
v. 9. Savings and Investment Options to Telecommuting--v. 10. Temporary Workers to Yamaha--
v. 11. Index volume
    ISBN 0-7614-7430-7 (set)--ISBN 0-7614-7438-2 (v. 8)
     1. Business--Encyclopedias. 2. Industries--Encyclopedias. I. Childs, William R., 1951-II. Martin,
Scott B., 1961-III. Stitt-Gohdes, Wanda.

HF1001 .B796 2003
338'.003--dc21   2002035156

Printed in Italy

06 05 04 03 5 4 3 2 1

MARSHALL CAVENDISH

Editorial Director	Paul Bernabeo
Production Manager	Alan Tsai

Produced by The Moschovitis Group, Inc.

THE MOSCHOVITIS GROUP

President, Publishing Division	Valerie Tomaselli
Executive Editor	Hilary W. Poole
Associate Editor	Sonja Matanovic
Design and Layout	Annemarie Redmond
Illustrator	Richard Garratt
Assistant Illustrator	Zahiyya Abdul-Karim
Photo Research	Gillian Speeth
Production Associates	K. Nura Abdul-Karim, Rashida Allen
Editorial Assistants	Christina Campbell, Nicole Cohen, Jessica Rosin
Copyediting	Carole Campbell
Proofreading	Paul Scaramazza
Indexing	AEIOU, Inc.

Alphabetical Table of Contents

Price Controls

Price controls are restrictions on prices used by governments to alter market outcomes. These controls typically take the form of a maximum price (a price ceiling) or minimum price (a price floor) in an individual market, although general price controls have sometimes been imposed in many markets simultaneously to try to contain inflation. Prices in markets are typically driven by supply and demand and have an important role in the efficient allocation of resources. However, markets do not necessarily lead to an equitable outcome for everyone, prompting policy makers to attempt to improve the market outcome.

The specific justification for intervention in a market may come from any of a number of sources, for example, concern for the welfare of the poor, the incomes of certain producers, or national security. Proponents of a higher minimum wage, for example, commonly cite the need for the working poor to earn enough to support themselves and their families. Milk price supports are typically justified by the need to generate adequate incomes for dairy farmers. Proponents of price protection for U.S. steel producers frequently stress the importance of a healthy domestic steel industry for national security. Economists are often skeptical about the social desirability of price controls and sometimes suggest that political expediency overrides genuine concerns about economic welfare when such controls are implemented.

A price ceiling is a legal maximum price that can be charged for a good or service. Governments impose price ceilings in markets where the prevailing price is perceived to be too high. Because the ceiling forces prices to be lower than they would be in an unregulated market, demand often outstrips supply: the quantity of the good or service supplied is often reduced while the quantity of the good or service demanded rises, usually resulting in a shortage. The intended beneficiary of the price ceiling is the consumer or purchaser of the good or service. Although some consumers may enjoy the benefit of the lower price, others may be left unable to secure the good or service at all. Black markets and other methods of evading the ceiling tend to develop as buyers look for ways to overcome the shortage and sellers accommodate them.

Rent control is a common example of a price ceiling. In some urban areas, rent control has been implemented to keep apartments affordable for people with limited incomes. Landlords may not be permitted to raise rent at all, or may be permitted to adjust rents only in small increments to stay even with the general inflation rate. Renters who are able to get rent-controlled apartments may benefit; however, price controls often have unintended negative consequences. In addition to a shortage of apartments and long waiting lists, some apartments may be taken off the market altogether as landlords convert buildings into condominiums or other uses not governed by the controls. Meanwhile, those buildings that remain apartments may be poorly maintained. With less rent coming

See also:
Agriculture Industry; Competition; Inflation; Minimum Wage; Monetary Policy; Subsidy.

Price Floors and Ceilings

Effects of Price Ceilings
Increases quantity demanded
Decreases quantity supplied
Market Shortage

Effects of Price Floors
Increases quantity supplied
Reduces quantity demanded
Market surplus

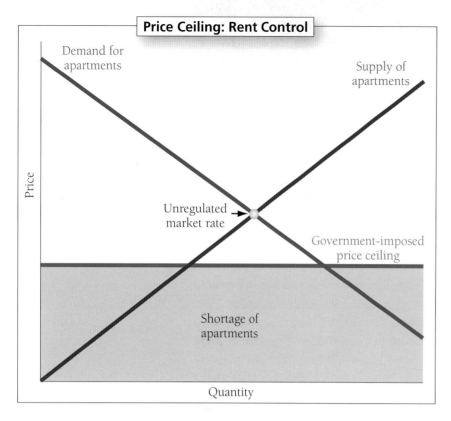

Price Ceiling: Rent Control

Demand for
apartments

Supply of
apartments

Price

Unregulated
market rate

Government-imposed
price ceiling

Shortage of
apartments

Quantity

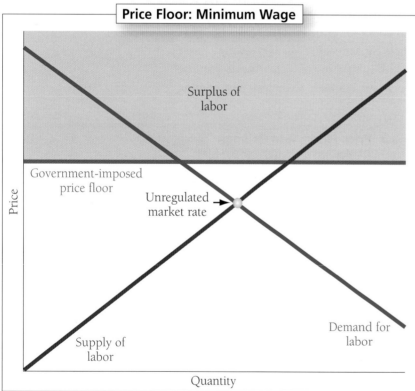

Price Floor: Minimum Wage

Surplus of
labor

Government-imposed
price floor

Unregulated
market rate

Price

Demand for
labor

Supply of
labor

Quantity

These charts show the theoretical basis for price ceilings and floors. Normally, market rates are established by the intersection of supply and demand. However, when the unregulated market rate is deemed to be too high (in the case of rent) or too low (in the case of wages), a government-imposed price can be established to lower rents or raise wages. The imposition of a price ceiling sometimes creates a shortage (as in the case of apartments); the imposition of a price floor sometimes creates a surplus (as in the case of labor).

in and a long line of prospective renters looking for apartments, building owners have less incentive to service and renovate buildings than they would in an unregulated competitive market.

A price floor is a legal minimum price that can be charged in a market. Governments impose price floors when the market price is perceived to be too low. The intention is to benefit producers or sellers of goods and services, although once again unintended negative consequences are possible. A price floor set above the market equilibrium typically creates a surplus of goods or services on the market as suppliers wish to sell more at the higher price while users cut back in response to the higher price. The resulting market glut either finds its way illegally to buyers at discount rates, moves to other unregulated markets, or leaves sellers with undesired inventories. In some cases—agricultural markets, for example—the government has supported the price floor by buying the surplus on the market.

A common price floor is a minimum wage law. In the United States, the federal government has imposed some form of a minimum wage since the Great Depression. Intended to help low-income workers, the minimum wage has undoubtedly boosted the pay of millions of workers since its implementation. Although the real purchasing power of the minimum wage has generally fallen since the 1960s, many workers still enjoy a higher wage than they might in the absence of the law.

However, the minimum wage can have undesirable consequences. Although some disagreement has been voiced, many economists believe that when the minimum wage is increased significantly above the wage level that would otherwise prevail in the labor market, the unemployment rate will rise because of the surplus of labor. Among the groups likely to be hurt by a rise in unemployment are teenagers and others just entering the labor force and those already most economically disadvantaged. Here economists point to the trade-offs inherent in policy making: raising the income of those

Apartment buildings on New York City's Upper West Side. New York State's rent regulation laws cover about 1.2 million apartments, housing more than 2.5 million tenants, mostly in the New York City area.

minimum-wage workers who keep their jobs may come not only at the expense of the businesses that pay them, but also at the expense of those who lose jobs or cannot find jobs at all.

When a government imposes a price control in a single market, such as the labor market via the minimum wage, it is trying to create an outcome that is more equitable or otherwise desirable than the market would generate independently. Sometimes governments intervene to regulate prices in markets that are not competitive in the first place. For example, many public utilities are "natural

Price Controls and the California Electricity Crisis

During the summer of 2000, price controls became a hot topic as California experienced a crisis in its electricity markets. On several occasions, demand for electrical power exceeded supply, resulting in sporadic blackouts in parts of the state. Along with power shortages, the wholesale price of electricity became extraordinarily volatile, peaking at hundreds of times its typical precrisis level.

With consumers at the retail level largely protected by a legal price ceiling, some utilities were caught in the middle, paying exorbitant prices to power generators but unable to recoup these costs from their customers. The state's largest utility, Pacific Gas and Electric (PG&E), declared bankruptcy. The state then spent billions of dollars purchasing electricity in the aftermath of the PG&E bankruptcy and the near-collapse of other utilities.

Supporters and critics of price controls interpret the crisis differently. Proponents of price controls for electricity blame the crisis on the deregulation of the wholesale power market several years earlier. They contend that if price caps had been in place in the wholesale market—in which utilities buy their power from generators—most of the financial crisis could have been averted. Opponents of price ceilings in electricity argue the opposite: had price caps been in place, they say, the shortages would have been even more severe and generators would have had less incentive to produce power. Furthermore, opponents of price controls argue, the cause of the financial crisis was not the soaring wholesale price but the price ceiling in the retail market, which failed to give consumers adequate incentive to reduce consumption.

monopolies"—industries in which having a single producer is more efficient than having many competing producers—and are typically regulated by the government.

In other areas, governments do not control prices directly but do exert influence on prices through taxes and subsidies. A subsidy, for example, will encourage increased production and lower prices to consumers, thus having an effect similar to a price ceiling without creating a shortage. However, the subsidy is costly to the government and therefore to taxpayers. In international trade, taxes on imports are called tariffs, and these tariffs can be used to protect domestic producers from foreign competition by increasing the price above what the market would otherwise dictate. For example, the steel industry in the United States has faced vigorous competition from foreign producers and has sought protection, citing its importance to national security and the need to keep workers employed.

Price controls are sometimes used by governments not to alter individual market outcomes but to control prices across the board. Such price controls are particularly enticing to policy makers during periods of high inflation. Nations worldwide have used price controls to limit inflation. In the United States, wage and price controls were attempted during the early 1970s by the Nixon administration. The root cause of inflation, however, is almost always the government's failure to control the growth of the money supply; thus price controls have typically had limited success. Although sometimes useful in the short run to slow the inflation rate, price controls can cause severe misallocations of resources and can stifle economic activity.

Prices play a critical role in a market economy because they indicate to consumers and producers where to allocate resources. High prices tell producers that a good or service is highly valued and that they should produce more, while also suggesting to consumers that a good or service is scarce and precious. However, high prices for necessities can hurt consumers, sometimes even as the producers make huge profits. A similar situation occurs with low prices: the market is signaling buyers to consume more and producers to make less—consumers benefit, but producers may suffer. In situations where price controls are contemplated, policy makers must typically weigh the trade-off between the desirability of a more equitable or socially acceptable outcome and the distortion of incentives that price controls create.

Further Reading

Borenstein, Severin. "The Trouble with Electricity Markets: Understanding California's Restructuring Disaster." *The Journal of Economic Perspectives* 16 (Winter 2002): 191–211.

Miller, Roger LeRoy, Daniel K. Benjamin, and Douglass C. North. *The Economics of Public Issues.* 12th ed. Boston: Addison-Wesley, 2001.

Swartz, Thomas R., and Frank J. Bonello, eds. *Taking Sides: Clashing Views on Controversial Economic Issues.* 10th ed. Guilford, Conn.: McGraw-Hill/Dushkin, 2002.

Thompson, Victor Alexander. *The Regulatory Process in OPA Rationing.* New York: Kings Crown Press, 1950.

—*Randall E. Waldron*

Price Fixing

Price fixing is a practice in which businesses enter into an agreement to collectively raise prices for their products. Most often price fixing is observed in oligopolies, which are markets controlled by several firms. Although not a monopoly, an oligopoly has a potential for bringing harm to consumers by limiting competition between the businesses in the market. Companies, in the pursuit of greater profits, have the incentive to raise their prices. However, for one company to raise its prices individually, without others following suit, is a poor strategy: its customers will quickly switch to purchasing its competitors' products at lower prices. Accordingly, raising prices must be a collective action.

Executives of competing companies can reach a formal agreement by actually holding meetings or negotiations; collusion can also be achieved implicitly, with firms "signaling" their intentions to each other. The latter kind of arrangement is also known as tacit collusion. Both kinds of collusive agreements are illegal in the United States, as is any attempt to restrict competition.

Theoretical Background

A price fixing scheme is difficult to sustain for a prolonged time. Indeed, attempts at collusion have failed on many occasions in many industries, and successful collusive arrangements are rare. However, certain conditions may make price fixing in a given industry more likely. Therefore, economists and policy makers must closely monitor markets that are susceptible to cartels.

The difficulty in sustaining collusive arrangements arises from three main aspects of price fixing. First, and probably most

See also:
AOL Time Warner; Cartel; Competition; Monopoly; Sherman Antitrust Act.

Competitors that sell products that are indistinguishable from each other, like concrete, are more likely to engage in price fixing schemes.

important, price fixing was made illegal by the Sherman Antitrust Act of 1890. Engaging in collusive behavior involves a great degree of risk for businesses, which may face substantial penalties if found guilty. Second, reaching the agreement may be difficult as it depends on the characteristics of a particular market. For example, such agreement may involve dividing the market into segments and specifying how much output each firm will supply in each segment. Third, price fixing conspiracies rarely survive because the members of the cartel tend to cheat on each other. Each firm would like to increase its profit at the expense of others; to that end, a business can slightly cut its price, which will entice the customers of other companies to switch to its product. Other firms will likely respond by cutting their prices as well, and the conspiracy will fall apart.

The fewer firms involved in a collusive scheme, the more likely it is to last. Clearly, coordinating the actions of two or three companies is much easier than coordinating the actions of seven or eight businesses. The relative sizes of firms may also be a factor: if one firm is clearly a dominant player in the market, it may act as a leader with the rest of the industry as followers. Similarly sized firms may have less incentive to cheat on the agreement because they may have similar amounts at stake.

Higher prices and greater profits resulting from the conspiracy will attract other entrants—firms not presently in the market. If significant entry barriers (costs that must be borne by each potential entrant) exist, then the price fixing scheme is more likely to be successful. For example, a group of dentists in a small rural community is likely to succeed at fixing prices because the obstacles involved in entering the market—one must be licensed to practice dentistry and have offices in the area—are formidable.

The more similar the products of the colluding firms, the easier the coordinating of their pricing and supplying actions. Thus, in the cement industry collusion is more likely than in the manufacture of furniture because cement produced by one company is completely substitutable for cement produced by another—not usually the case with furniture. Also, the degree to which demand for the cartel's product responds to an increase in price will play a role in determining whether a collusion survives. If the firms are able to raise prices without losing too many customers—for example, because customers switch to substitutes or stop buying altogether—then price fixing is more likely to occur in this market. Economists refer to such demand as inelastic: it is not very sensitive to price changes.

Certain aspects of an industry make cheating by one of the colluding firms easily detectable and punishable, in which case such factors serve as a deterrent to cheating. In other words, if there is a greater chance of getting caught, a firm is less likely to engage in cheating, even though there is a substantial benefit to such behavior. For example, if all firms sell their products only through their catalogs and Web sites, then their prices can be easily checked by their competitors; hence, cheating is difficult and unlikely. If, however, firms are able to give secret, unpublished discounts to their customers in

CD Price Fixing

In August 2000, 41 states filed an antitrust lawsuit against five of the largest music companies: Universal Music, Sony Music, Warner Music, Bertelsmann's BMG Music, and EMI Group. It was argued that these companies, in collaboration with music retailers throughout the country, were involved in a questionable plan to keep CD prices artificially high between 1995 and 2000. They were accused of practicing Minimum Advertised Pricing (MAP), whereby music companies offer to subsidize advertising for retail stores in return for an agreement to sell the CDs at a higher price.

The music companies admitted no wrongdoing, claiming that their MAP practices made it possible for smaller retail stores to compete with larger outlet stores, such as Wal-Mart and Target. They argued that huge chains can afford to drastically cut CD prices to attract customers, which in turn harms small retailers. A representative of Universal stated, "We believe our policies were pro-competitive and geared towards keeping more retailers, large and small, in business."

Nevertheless, citing large litigation fees, the companies agreed to a settlement in which they would pay $67.4 million in cash to compensate consumers who overpaid for CDs in the years in question. Any person who purchased a CD between 1995 and 2000 could apply to receive a portion of the settlement. In addition, these companies agreed to distribute $75.7 million worth of CDs to public entities and nonprofit organizations throughout the country. According to New York attorney general Eliot Spitzer, the case is a "landmark settlement to address years of illegal price fixing."

—Nicole Cohen

their stores, then detecting such behavior is difficult and cheating may occur.

Examples of Price Fixing

The early cases brought by the U.S. government under the Sherman Act were considered to be the government's first steps in antitrust enforcement, in which the interpretation of the vague language of the laws was revealed. For example, in *United States v. Addyston Pipe and Steel Co.* (1898), the defendants were found guilty of a price fixing conspiracy in the cast-iron pipe market in southern and western states. The firms, which controlled about 65 percent of the cast-iron pipe production in the market, kept their prices just low enough to discourage entry by the firms from the eastern states. This case had tremendous significance for the future of antitrust enforcement: in its decision, the court established that price fixing was per se illegal, that is, illegal even if not unreasonably high or not resulting in substantial consumer harm.

Some antitrust cases are brought by private parties rather than by the government. In 1986 Zenith, a U.S. maker of electronics, sued Matsushita and several other Japanese companies for allegedly engaging in a price fixing conspiracy in the United States in an attempt to drive American firms out of business. The case alleged that the Japanese makers of televisions entered into a two-phase agreement, under which their prices were to be kept very low in the first phase and high in the second. The first phase, during which the conspirators may sustain considerable financial losses, is designed to gain control of the market by eliminating competition; the second is the recoupment stage, when prices are set high so that the resulting profits are at least enough to offset the losses. After examining the evidence, the court concluded that the plaintiff had no grounds for the accusations of low-price conspiracy—if anything, the Japanese appeared to have engaged in a high-price conspiracy. However, even this possible high-price scheme was unsuccessful because individual Japanese firms cheated on the

alleged agreement, rendering it ineffective. The court dismissed the case.

Recent Price Fixing Cases

Two major allegations of price fixing were made famous by the media in 2000 and 2001. One case involved the world's two largest auction houses, Sotheby's and Christie's, which were charged with fixing the fees that they charge sellers. The two rival companies, which specialize in art auctions, were found guilty of colluding for more than six years, beginning in 1993. Their conspiracy effectively eliminated competition between them and cost their customers millions of dollars.

The other case involved a somewhat more subtle agreement between two competitors, who shared ownership of a unique product. AOL Time Warner and Vivendi, two of the major recording studios, jointly marketed the audio and video products from the recording of the Three Tenors performance at the 1998 World Cup soccer finals in Paris. Each company also had exclusive

A 1986 lawsuit brought by a U.S. television manufacturer alleged that some Japanese companies were engaged in a price fixing scheme; the court found the Japanese companies to be innocent and the case was dismissed.

A Christie's auctioneer takes a bid on the painting Nature morte aux tulipes *by Pablo Picasso, on sale at Christie's 20th Century Art Sale in New York in 2000. The auction took place under the cloud of a federal price fixing investigation of both Christie's and its British rival, Sotheby's.*

rights to market a previous performance release—Vivendi distributed the 1990 concert products, and Warner sold the 1994 performance. In 1998 the two companies agreed to collaborate on the marketing of the third series of recordings. Because they feared that the 1998 recordings would not be as popular with the public as the previous releases, the firms entered into an agreement not to advertise or give discounts on their Three Tenors audio and video products for several months. Effectively, such actions do not differ from fixing prices on their solely owned products; the Federal Trade Commission threatened a lawsuit. AOL Time Warner immediately settled, agreeing to discontinue the objectionable behavior.

Armed with the tools of modern economic theory and several decades of experience, the antitrust authorities are now better equipped to monitor and prosecute anticompetitive behavior than they were in the past. Although these tools make a price fixing conspiracy even less likely to survive, many

do, as is clear from the case of Christie's and Sotheby's, which colluded undetected for several years.

Further Reading

Borenstein, Severin. "Rapid Price Communication and Coordination: The Airline Tariff Publishing Case." In *The Antitrust Revolution: Economics, Competition, and Policy,* edited by John Kwoka and Lawrence White. 3rd ed. New York: Oxford University Press, 1999.

Breit, William, and Kenneth Elzinga. *The Antitrust Casebook: Milestones in Economic Regulation.* 3rd ed. Fort Worth, Tex.: Dryden Press, 1996.

Elzinga, Kenneth. "Collusive Predation: Matsushita v. Zenith." In *The Antitrust Revolution: Economics, Competition, and Policy,* edited by John Kwoka and Lawrence White. 3rd ed. New York: Oxford University Press, 1999.

O'Sullivan, Arthur, and Steven M. Sheffrin. *Microeconomics: Principles and Tools.* 2nd ed. Upper Saddle River, N.J.: Prentice Hall, 2001.

—*Mikhail Kouliavtsev*

Pricing

Economics may seem abstract, but everyone knows what a price is. The Consumer Price Index, a compilation of prices of common goods and services, is the subject of as much media attention as the unemployment rate. Rising prices can decimate a nation's economy; falling prices can do even worse damage. Governments regularly intervene to manipulate prices, either directly through price controls or indirectly by altering interest rates to control inflation.

How are prices actually set? In theory, pricing is simple: companies want to charge as high a price as they can because that increases profits, while consumers want to pay as little as possible. The price set is a compromise, affected mainly by the scarcity of the item.

The real world, however, is much more complicated. According to the law of demand, demand for a product should go up when the price is reduced. In reality, sales of certain products will actually increase if the price is raised—the exact opposite of what the law of demand predicts. Indeed, the best-selling brands of a particular good are usually priced somewhat higher than competitive brands. Under the right circumstances, people under no duress will pay more for the same product that is readily available elsewhere for less. Not surprisingly, psychologists have as much to say about pricing as economists.

Setting Prices

Setting the right price is a balancing act. Companies want to charge as much as possible; however, if prices are set too high, not enough customers will buy the product for the company to be profitable. If the company sets prices too low, the company will receive less for the item than it cost to produce—and the more people buying the item, the more money lost.

The cost of production is sometimes the main consideration in pricing. For example, a traditional regulated utility has a monopoly on a vital service—for example, providing electricity in a particular state. To protect consumers, state regulators set the prices the utility may charge customers. Those prices are usually based on the cost to the utility of providing electricity, plus a profit. If the utility wishes to raise rates, it must convince regulators that its costs have increased or will soon do so.

In most cases, cost is only one consideration when a company sets a price; often cost is far from the most important factor. The cost of producing a good usually serves as a lower limit to its price, but sometimes a company will deliberately set prices below the cost of production and lose money on sales. Often this step is taken as part of a larger strategy to raise cash, enter a new market, or undermine competitors.

The competitive environment often has a much larger effect on pricing than does the cost of production. If two companies are offering two very similar products, one business may decide to undercut the other on price. That action may trigger what is called a price war, with competitors cutting prices until all are selling the product for less than it cost to produce. Like a real war, the object of a price war is usually to kill the enemy; whichever company is in better financial shape will survive.

When many companies offer essentially the same product, price wars are common, and prices generally settle at a level that is only slightly above the cost of making the product—a situation called commodity pricing. When commodity pricing becomes the norm in an industry,

See also:
Advertising, Business Practice; Brand Names; Competition; Consumer Price Index; Market Research; Price Controls; Price Fixing; Supply and Demand.

Factors Involved in Pricing	
Market factors	Customer behavior and preferences
	Competitive environment
	Cost
Corporate factors	Product positioning
	Marketing strategy
	Regulation and taxes

Ministers of the Organization of Petroleum Exporting Countries (OPEC) meeting at OPEC headquarters in Vienna in 2000.

weaker competitors tend to go out of business, merge, or get bought by stronger companies. The shakeout produces a few strong players who control most of the market and thus have more power to raise prices. Profits in commodity businesses, nevertheless, tend to be small.

Prices can be set higher, however, if a single company, a monopoly, takes over the entire market. A monopoly has no competitors to undercut its prices, so it can keep prices high and be very profitable. Higher prices do not benefit consumers, however, so the monopolies can run afoul of antitrust laws, which are designed to ensure competition. Whether a monopoly has legal trouble depends on the market it controls and how it responds to attempts by other companies to enter that market.

An equally effective method of preventing commodity prices from declining is for companies to collude to keep prices high, a practice called price fixing. Price fixing is illegal in the United States; nonetheless it occurs regularly—surreptitiously within the country and openly outside of it. The OPEC oil cartel, for example, is a group of oil-producing nations that meet periodically and agree on how much oil they will produce, which essentially fixes the price of oil (although some OPEC nations cheat and produce more oil than they have agreed to—a common problem among price fixers).

Companies that become monopolies or fix prices may run afoul of the law. However, a completely legal method to avoid the downward spiral of commodity pricing

Effect of Commodity Pricing

Many companies offer same product.

⬇

Price wars ensue.

⬇

Price settles slightly above cost (commodity pricing).

⬇

Weaker competitors fail, merge, or are bought.

⬇

A few strong players emerge.

⬇

The few players raise prices.

exists: prevent the product from becoming a commodity. A good example is personal computers (PCs). IBM-compatible PCs, which are made by many different manufacturers, are all very similar and have, in pricing terms, become a commodity. Personal computers made by Apple remain expensive. Unlike PCs, Apple computers are made only by Apple, and they differ in many ways from PCs, which insulates Apple from price wars in the PC market. For example, Apple computers are considered easier to use than PCs, which makes them popular with schools. They also handle graphics well, which makes them popular with design professionals. Educators and design professionals who believe that Apple computers are better than PCs are willing to pay more, so Apple can keep its prices high.

Apple Computer CEO Steve Jobs introducing the new iMac in 1997. Apple's small but devoted fan base and its one-of-a-kind products make Macs somewhat price insensitive.

This approach has drawbacks. Apple is a relatively small company with only a small share of the personal computer market; Apple must be relentlessly innovative to justify its higher price and keep customers loyal. Nonetheless, Apple's approach has helped it to survive for more than 20 years, a significant achievement in the volatile computer industry.

The Psychology of Pricing

What keeps Apple viable is that consumers, under the right circumstances, will pay higher prices and in some cases would rather pay more. Why people will pay more, who will pay more for what, and how much more they are willing to pay are subjects that keep countless marketers, advertisers, psychologists, and economists gainfully employed. Successful companies find the right mix of intangibles that make people willing to accept higher prices, and then set prices at the appropriately higher level.

Whether consumers will find a particular price acceptable can be hard to predict. The way prices are presented can make a difference. Retailers tend to use odd pricing—pricing a good at $3.99 rather than $4.00—which makes consumers more likely to think they are getting a bargain.

```
┌─────────────────────────────┐
│   Psychological Factors     │
│        in Pricing           │
├─────────────────────────────┤
│  • Quality                  │
│  • Convenience              │
│  • Value                    │
│  • Social status in luxury goods │
└─────────────────────────────┘
```

Likewise, consumers are more willing to find a price acceptable if they believe it has been discounted from a higher price. Consumers are more accepting of high prices for optional items like desserts and fancy shoes than for necessities like electricity. Even the same goods—soda or candy, for instance—can command vastly higher prices in an entertainment venue like a movie theater than in an ordinary setting like a grocery store.

One of the reasons people do not always seek the lowest price is that most people do not really know exactly what prices they pay for goods—even goods they buy fairly regularly. People tend to think in terms of price ranges. They have an upward limit of what they would be willing to spend for a particular item, and they also have a downward limit—if an item is priced below that limit, people tend to assume something is wrong with it. The acceptable price range for a product can shift over time to reflect, for example, inflation or the falling price of aging technology.

Customers may also be willing to pay a higher price for a good if they believe they are receiving more value. What is perceived as value depends on the individual buyer. However, groups of people tend to share similar attitudes about what constitutes value. Such a group is known as a market segment or market niche, and successful products and brands usually target a particular segment very carefully.

One kind of value is convenience. For example, people will pay a good deal more for food that has already been prepared and cooked than for food that they must prepare and cook themselves. Drugstores have increased revenues by expanding the kinds of goods they carry to include items like

Pricing Airline Tickets

Until the late 1970s the airline industry in the United States was heavily regulated, not only for safety but also in all aspects. Federal regulators set ticket prices, and the vast majority of travelers paid the full fare. That is no longer the case: ticket prices vary widely, and the vast majority of travelers get some form of discount. Prices and profit margins on different routes vary considerably, usually depending on how many carriers fly the route.

Ticket prices can vary widely even for the same route. Fly tourist class from New York City to London in January, and a round-trip ticket could cost less than $200. Fly the same route business class, and the ticket could cost more than $6,000.

Market segmentation is one cause of this price differential. Tourists, by definition, do not need to fly to London—they could go anywhere. Consequently, the price of the flight must be low, otherwise very few people will choose to vacation in London and the flight will have lots of empty seats. Businesspeople, on the other hand, travel because they must, and, as their company is paying the price of the ticket, they are far less sensitive to price. Businesspeople are also far more likely than tourists to need to travel at the last minute and to stay in their destination for only a few days. The tourist, who buys well in advance and stays longer, benefits from the airline's need to plan because the airline will offer cheaper fares in return for certain profit.

groceries. Milk may cost more at a drug-store than at a grocery store, but many people will pay the premium if it saves them a trip to another store.

A broad market segment values quality. Quality, like value, means different things to different people, but generally it guarantees that an item will last, will not break, and will effectively do the job it is designed to do. As most people equate higher price with higher quality, people who value quality expect to pay higher prices. Most best-selling brands market themselves as providing better quality for a slightly higher price.

Sometimes the higher price itself is the appeal because some people want the social status that is attached to being able to buy something very expensive. Luxury brands that sell to such status-oriented people must be priced very carefully to ensure that their prices do not become too low, or they will "go downmarket" and alienate their core market segment.

If a maker of luxury goods does not protect its brand from going downmarket, its goods might get caught between market segments, which is never good. Say the House of Swank makes hand-embroidered silk shirts that are sold at high-end boutiques for $600 and are coveted by socialites and social climbers everywhere. The House of Swank does not pay too much attention to distribution, and pretty soon Swank shirts are available at outlet malls for $200. Word gets around that Swank shirts might not cost as much as previously believed. Soon wearing one becomes a faux pas among the status-conscious, and, as no one else is willing to shell out $600 for a shirt, sales of Swank in high-end boutiques grind to a halt.

The market share that shops in outlet malls, however, is still the wrong crowd for House of Swank. Outlet-mall shoppers are looking for bargains—$20 shirts, not $200 ones. Swank shirts are thus too cheap for the status-conscious and too expensive for the budget-minded. Swank cannot sell in the boutiques, it cannot sell in the outlet

The Internet Browser Price War

In the spring of 1996, Netscape's Navigator was king of Web-browsing software, which allows users to access the World Wide Web. Navigator controlled almost 90 percent of the market largely because of an innovative pricing strategy that Netscape executives called "free, but not free." Navigator was available as a free download from the Internet for 90 days. After that, users were supposed to pay. Many casual users never did, but corporate users, who wanted technical support along with the software, usually did pay. In addition, wide distribution of Navigator promoted sales of Netscape's lucrative server software.

However, Microsoft, which makes the operating systems used on the vast majority of PCs, began giving away its own browser, Explorer, for free when people purchased the Windows operating systems on a new computer that had Windows already installed. For most users, Navigator was also free from a monetary standpoint, but it had another cost—the time and effort spent to download it.

Navigator began to lose market share rapidly, and in early 1998 Netscape made it truly free. The loss of revenues from this policy hurt Netscape financially, and the company failed to upgrade its browser. Netscape was acquired in late 1998 by America Online, but its browser effectively became obsolete, leaving Explorer to dominate the market.

malls, and pretty soon the House of Swank, a victim of poor pricing, is out of business.

Pricing remains more of an art than a science and will probably always have an element of unpredictability. Indeed, the prices people are willing to pay are so difficult for others to predict that some economists point to auctions as a sort of ultimate solution to the quandaries of pricing. Instead of having marketers, regulators, and economists attempt to determine a good price, auctions allow consumers to set their own price, and their reasons for picking that price remain their own.

Further Reading

Dolan, Robert J., and Hermann Simon. *Power Pricing: How Managing Price Transforms the Bottom Line.* New York: Free Press, 1996.

Engelson, Morris. *Pricing Strategy: An Interdisciplinary Approach.* Portland, Ore.: Joint Management Strategy, 1995.

Morris, Michael H., and Gene Morris. *Market Oriented Pricing: Strategies for Management.* New York: Quorum Books, 1990.

Nagle, Thomas T., and Reed K. Holden. *The Strategy and Tactics of Pricing: A Guide to Profitable Decision Making.* 3rd ed. Upper Saddle River, N.J.: Prentice Hall, 2002.

Weiss, Leonard W., ed. *Concentration and Price.* Cambridge, Mass.: MIT Press, 1989.

Winkler, John. *Pricing for Results.* New York: Facts On File, 1984.

—*Mary Sisson*

Private Property

Property consists of the rights to particular entities, tangible or intangible, that allow the rights holders to engage in transactions, or not, according to their own desires. Property can consist of tangible objects, for example, a book or land, or intangibles, for instance, the ideas expressed in a book or the design of an invention. Private property is property held by individuals, either singly or in voluntary associations, rather than that held by the state.

Traditionally, private property rights include the rights to exclude others, to transfer the property, and to receive the benefits of owning the property. Property rights are almost infinitely divisible, however, and changes in social norms, private behavior, and public rules can result in changes in private property rights. For example, when a city adopts a zoning code, landowners lose some of their property rights to the city, because the landowners are now restricted in their use of their land in ways that they were not before the code was passed.

Private property rights have a long history in Western societies. Property rights to land, for example, were a crucial part of the feudal system instituted by William the Conqueror in England in 1066, and much of English history for the next several centuries can be interpreted as a struggle between the English Crown and the nobility over control of those rights. Some authors argue that the existence of private property in England was critical to the development of political freedom. Historian Richard Pipes, for example, compares England with Tsarist Russia, where secure private property did not exist. Pipes explains the absence of liberty in Russia as a consequence of the absence of private property.

Sources of Property Rights

Where do property rights come from? One tradition, drawing on the work of seventeenth-century philosopher John Locke, argues that property rights are natural rights, meaning that they are innate and stem from nature rather than being granted by a sovereign. Another tradition, based on the work of another seventeenth-century philosopher, Thomas Hobbes, argues that property rights depend on the existence of a government to secure them. Modern writers have often used economic theory to locate private property rights in voluntary arrangements among individuals.

The Lockean tradition rests on the idea that individuals can withdraw material from the common pool of unclaimed assets (for example, fish from the ocean) by mixing their labor with those assets. Thus a fisherman who casts a net into the ocean owns the fish caught because of his efforts. The Hobbesian tradition, on the other hand, argues that because the supply of fish is limited, conflict will erupt between individuals over who can withdraw fish from the sea. Only the government can prevent such conflict from erupting into a war of all against all by limiting individuals' claims on property.

The question of where property rights arise is important. If property rights exist independently of the state, then the ability of governments to take property away from individuals has limits. If, on the other hand, property rights are merely privileges granted by the state, then few restrictions are in place on governments in abrogating individuals' property rights.

Crucial Roles of Private Property in Capitalism

- Creates incentives to maximize value of property
- Encourages exercise of good stewardship of property
- Allows the organization of productive activities without interference from others
- Results in increases in the value of property, which can fund investment

The most basic form of private property: a piece of land.

The Role of Private Property

Private property serves several important functions. First, because the owner of property reaps the rewards of proper stewardship and suffers the losses of wasteful actions, private property gives individuals the incentive to care for their property responsibly. For example, if a farmer overuses her agricultural land, its value will decline. If, however, she cares for the land properly, it will increase in value. In either case, the property owner suffers the losses and reaps the rewards. Farmland that is shared among many people is likely to have poorer stewardship because good care may not benefit the prudent farmer; rather, someone else may benefit.

Second, private property rights provide boundaries within which individuals can live their lives free from the interference of others. Delineating a property boundary between neighbors makes clear where one person's exercise of rights is allowable and another's is not, and so reduces conflict. Private property rights also give individuals an important degree of

> **New Kinds of Personal Property**
>
> - Airwaves
> - DNA
> - Organs and body parts
> - Personal information
> - Personal image

political independence from the state, allowing them to resist authoritarian rulers.

Third, private property allows individuals to accumulate wealth, which can then be invested. In the United States, for example, the clear delineation of property rights allows landowners to tap their wealth through mortgages and other financial instruments, raising capital that can be used to invest. To accomplish mortgages, loans, rentals, and sales, the right to transfer property and thereby capture changes in value is critical. In countries without secure private property rights, however, wealth in land remains trapped. As a result, economic development is stalled and the society remains poor.

Finally, private property rights give people the incentive to protect their property over time, so that owners may pass their property to their descendants or to whomever they will. Private property owners, accordingly, have an incentive to preserve and raise the value of their property through careful stewardship. This contrasts sharply with the behavior of those who control property through political means, whose incentive is to extract as much value as possible from the property while they control it.

Through these four functions, private property plays a critical role in capitalism. Indeed, capitalism is impossible without private property because without it, no incentive exists for those who control resources to innovate, to produce more than can be immediately consumed, or to treat resources wisely. Private ownership creates incentives to maximize the value of property and to exercise good stewardship of it, allows the organization of productive activities without interference from others, and results in

increases in the value of property, which can fund investment.

The Economics of Private Property

Property rights can be established in varying degrees of detail. Consider the difference between the property right established by a movie theater ticket and a ticket to a Broadway play. The movie ticket allows the holder to sit in a seat in the theater during a specific performance; the theater ticket allows the holder to sit in a particular seat during a specific performance.

To protect the property rights of the theater ticket holder, the theater owner must invest in ensuring that no more than one ticket is sold for each seat, in ushers to ensure that the ticket holder can use her seat, and in markings on the seats. In contrast, the movie theater owner need invest in ensuring only that the number of tickets sold for any performance does not exceed the number of seats and that ticket holders do not enter the wrong theater. Because the theater owner can sell good seats for a higher price than bad seats, spending the additional money to better specify the property right makes economic sense.

This example illustrates a principle that applies broadly: As property rights become more valuable, people will invest more resources in better specifying those rights. Economists who study property rights use such concepts to examine how the allocation and definition of property rights affect issues as varied as the organizational structure of businesses and the behavior of people in rationing plans.

Opposition to Private Property

A long tradition of opposition to private property is associated with authoritarian regimes and thinkers: socialist, communist, or fascist. In his 1840 essay "What Is Property," Pierre-Joseph Proudhon, a French anarchist, coined the phrase "property is theft." Karl Marx, the father of modern communism, attacked the "vileness of private property." More recently, fascist thinkers argued that individual property owners must subordinate their property to the needs of the state. Such opposition is sometimes based on discomfort with the inequalities private ownership of property allows but also reflects a desire to prevent the political independence that private property ownership creates.

In the United States private property has come under attack primarily from environmentalists who argue that the problem is not inequality among people but individuals' failure to behave responsibly toward the natural world. Rather than allowing an individual to determine how to make use of a piece of land, these critics argue that society as a whole should determine how the land should be used. For example, an individual with an endangered species present on her property should not be able to take actions that might harm the endangered species.

Property Rights Issues for the Future

Property rights issues in the past largely arose around rights to land, water, and other tangible objects. As a result, an enormous body of law and other forms of knowledge concerning such forms of private property rights grew up and is available to assist with future questions about tangible property. Much more difficult are questions involving intellectual property: patent rights, trademark rights, copyright, and the like; intangible property, such as airwaves; and property that has only recently become valuable—human body parts, for instance.

Intellectual property rights differ from property rights to tangible objects in several important ways. Land cannot be duplicated, for example, while new technologies make the subject matter of copyright cheaply and perfectly reproducible. Similarly, no more than one person can occupy a particular physical location, while multiple people can listen to or read the same copyrighted material simultaneously without affecting others' use of the material.

New forms of property are also appearing in nontraditional places. With the increased ability for organ transplantation made possible by advances in medical technology, human body parts have acquired value. Do individuals own their bodies and, if so, can they sell off parts of them either before or after death?

A kidney arrives by plane in Rome for a transplant operation in 1993.

Would recognizing such rights increase the supply of organs for transplant, or would it dehumanize society, or both?

Advances in information technology permit much information about individuals to be exploited. Credit card companies, for example, are able to gather and use valuable knowledge about card holders by examining their spending patterns. Does this information belong to the card holder or the card company? The answers to such questions differ depending on the perceived basis for property rights, the importance of incentive effects on rights holders, and many other factors.

Further Reading

Barzel, Yoram. *Economic Analysis of Property Rights.* 2nd ed. Cambridge: Cambridge University Press, 1997.

Bethell, Tom. *The Noblest Triumph: Property and Prosperity through the Ages.* New York: St. Martin's Press, 1998.

De Soto, Hernando. *The Mystery of Capital.* New York: Basic Books, 2000.

Ely, James W., Jr. *The Guardian of Every Other Right: A Constitutional History of Property Rights.* 2nd ed. New York: Oxford University Press, 1998.

Pipes, Richard. *Property and Freedom.* New York: Alfred Knopf, 1999.

Simpson, A. W. B. *A History of the Land Law.* 2nd ed. Oxford: Clarendon Press, 1986.

—*Andrew Morriss*

Privatization

Privatization is the shift of government functions and assets into the private sector. Examples of privatization include replacing municipal garbage collection services with a private contractor, selling of ownership of a state industry or other asset to a private business or individual, and contracting with a private business to operate a state asset, as when a resort firm is hired to manage a state park. Privatization is important to businesses because it creates opportunities to expand and eliminates subsidized competition. Since the 1970s tens of thousands of enterprises throughout the world have been privatized.

Advantages of Privatization

The major advantage of privatization is the profit incentive. Because private businesses suffer losses and earn profits, they have incentives to manage assets efficiently. A manager whose division earns a profit, for example, often receives additional compensation or a promotion. Employees and managers of state-owned enterprises, on the other hand, are generally not subject to market discipline, and so lack those incentives. In particular, because civil service public sector employees and managers generally are compensated and promoted based on longevity of service rather than success, they lack the incentives to aggressively seek to lower costs that are present in private businesses.

State-owned and -operated enterprises are also subject to political interference. For example, a government may agree to raise wages for state workers to avoid labor unrest before an election, or it may divert investments or contracts to satisfy important constituents. Moving assets and services to the private sector can avoid many of these problems.

Another potential benefit of privatization is that it can force asset owners to face opportunity costs. For example, the Audubon Society owns a wildlife refuge in Louisiana where it has contracted for oil and gas production; Audubon uses the resulting profits to fund its wildlife preservation activities. However, the group opposes oil and gas production in the Arctic National Wildlife Refuge (ANWR).

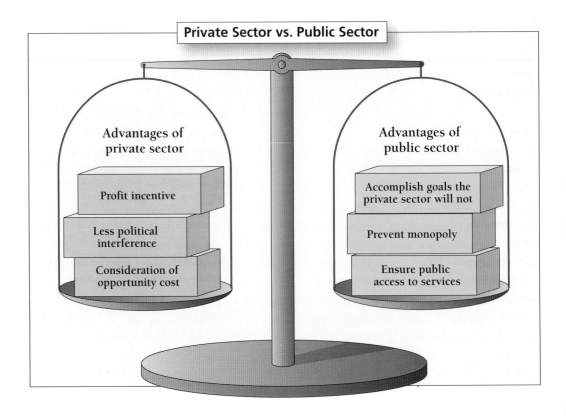

Private Sector vs. Public Sector

Advantages of private sector
- Profit incentive
- Less political interference
- Consideration of opportunity cost

Advantages of public sector
- Accomplish goals the private sector will not
- Prevent monopoly
- Ensure public access to services

British prime minister Margaret Thatcher, a leader of the privatization movement, in 1979.

On its own land, the environmental organization faced the opportunity cost of not exploiting the resources. On public land, however, those costs are borne by society as a whole, and the resource decision on public land must be made through political processes. When assets are held privately, decision makers must take opportunity costs into account.

Disadvantages of Privatization

State ownership of assets and provision of services is usually done to achieve specific goals. Privatization of some services and assets can frustrate accomplishment of the original goals. For example, many cities and towns in the United States created municipally owned public utilities to provide electricity because they feared investor-owned utilities would charge monopoly prices. Likewise, many local governments are investigating public ownership of broadband Internet networks within their borders and leasing the capacity to private businesses to prevent private cable companies from gaining

a monopoly. State ownership is one means of preventing monopoly profits.

State provision of services is often justified as necessary in cases where little profit is to be made—for example, to ensure access to particular services for the poor. Public primary and secondary education ensures public access to education without regard to income. (State ownership of schools is not required to achieve this goal, however, as the provision of vouchers and tax credits can enable underserved groups to gain access to privately provided services.) State ownership does provide greater public control of the content of education, however.

Strategies for Privatization

Studies by organizations like the World Bank have largely concluded that privatization can be beneficial when conducted properly. Private ownership of former state enterprises in both rich and poor countries has led to significant increases in profitability, service quality, service levels, and growth. Privatization of municipal services in the United States has produced increased productivity and quality of service. Not all privatizations are successful, however. Properly conducting privatization is key to its success. Among the most important factors are the following.

Rule of law. Privatization is successful only when the privatized business can operate in a market economy, which requires the rule of law. Privatized businesses must be able to rely on contracts and remain free of political interference.

Recognition of implicit property rights. Many interest groups feel they "own" state assets. A successful privatization must recognize these implicit claims on the assets when they are privatized. For example, one of the most successful privatizations was Prime Minister Margaret Thatcher's transfer of British public housing units to private ownership. Recognizing that the current tenants of the public housing felt they "owned" the right to remain in their homes, the Thatcher government privatized the units by offering to sell them at a discount to the tenants. By giving the tenants a good deal, the government converted these holders of implicit rights from potential opponents into supporters of privatization.

Avoiding overfragmentation of property rights. If privatization results in too many individuals holding claims to an asset, they may be unable to agree on how to manage their new property. For example, in Russia shares in many state enterprises were distributed to employees, managers, suppliers, customers, and other groups. The result was that each group was able to block the others from making use of the asset but was unable to implement its own preferred use, leaving many commercial buildings empty while new businesses operated from street kiosks.

Ensuring competitive market results. Simply transferring a monopoly firm or service from a public monopoly to a private monopoly may worsen the incentive problems, particularly if no regulatory structure is created to restrain the monopoly. Privatization of assets requires preprivatization division of the assets into small enough units to ensure no private monopoly results. In Britain's privatization of electricity generation plants, for example, the result was an oligopoly in generation rather than a competitive market because the government sold the plants in large groups rather than individually.

Ensuring fairness in the transfer. In theory, many of the benefits of privatization could be achieved by transferring state assets and services to any private owner. In practice,

Bolivian coca growers and union activists march on the road near Quemalia in 2001. Demonstrators demanded that the government reverse the privatization of state companies.

however, privatization is often politically impossible unless assets are fairly distributed. Many privatizations in formerly socialist countries have foundered because state ownership was replaced by "crony capitalism" in which politically well-connected individuals and groups secured former state assets at bargain basement prices.

Current Issues in Privatization

With the collapse of the Soviet Union and the revelation that Soviet claims of economic growth were false, support for direct state ownership of industrial resources also collapsed. As a result, much of current debate concerns how to privatize state-owned resources and whether to shift provision of services traditionally provided by state agencies into the private sector rather than whether private ownership is desirable.

One key debate centers on whose claims should be recognized in the privatization process. Should an enterprise be given to its employees, sold to the highest bidder, or allocated to all citizens through stock distributions? What should be done with the revenue generated by privatization? Should the new owner have responsibility for the enterprises' past conduct (for example, pollution) or have a clean slate? How should the transition be managed to minimize disruption of communities? All these questions require careful analysis and planning if privatization is to succeed.

In the United States, with relatively few state-owned enterprises, privatization has largely been discussed in terms of shifting service provision to the private sector to improve services. Proponents of education vouchers, for example, tout the benefits of a competitive education sector. Private investment of retirement accounts is offered as an alternative to social security. Municipalities consider shifting street repair, garbage collection, and other services to private firms. Almost any state service can be privatized by contracting with companies in the private sector. The question is: Do particular services have a sufficiently public character to justify their provision by the government?

Each privatization proposal must be justified individually. Many municipal privatizations in the United States fail because conditions are imposed that are designed to protect current employees' jobs; these conditions prevent the privatized entity from reducing labor costs. Although privatization has successfully transformed many state services and enterprises, it remains controversial. Successful privatization requires careful consideration of economic, regulatory, and political factors.

Public services like garbage pickup are often cited as good candidates for privatization.

Further Reading

Anderson, Terry L., and Peter J. Hill, eds. *The Privatization Process: A Worldwide Perspective*. Lanham, Md.: Rowman & Littlefield, 1996.

Bailey, Elizabeth E., and Janet Rothenberg Pack, eds. *The Political Economy of Privatization and Deregulation*. Brookfield, Vt.: Edward Elgar, 1995.

Vickers, John, and George Yarrow. *Privatization: An Economic Analysis*. Cambridge, Mass.: MIT Press, 1988.

Yergin, Daniel, and Joseph Stanislaw. *The Commanding Heights: The Battle between Government and the Marketplace That Is Remaking the Modern World*. New York: Simon & Schuster, 1998.

—*Andrew Morriss*

See also:
Business Plan; Distribution Channels; License; Patent; Research and Development; Supply and Demand; Trademark.

Product Development

Product development is the process of turning science into business or market research into market share. An individual or company takes an idea and turns it into a salable product. Products can be breakthrough products, for example, Apple's original computer, which was the first mass-marketed personal computer. It is considered a breakthrough product because it spawned a whole new market and way of life. Others, the wide-mouth toaster, for instance, are upgrades or improvements to existing products. Still others might be existing products in a new package, for example, pantyhose that comes in a plastic egg, or next-generation products like the change from cordless to wireless in telephones.

Product Development Cycle

Depending upon the product, various kinds of research are necessary to even begin thinking about creating a new product. Research is an information-gathering mission. Some very basic questions are: Will anyone want this product? Does the product solve a problem or, if it is a new product, will it improve quality of life? Two basic categories of research are market research, for example, questioning consumers about the proposed product or about problems with existing products, and scientific research, for example, finding a way to produce higher-quality sound recordings. Ideas for products can come from both.

The design phase, which follows scientific and market research, is the beginning of serious decision making. Who is the target market? Should the product be aimed at a high-end market willing to pay for superior quality or should it be aimed at the low-end market using the lowest-cost materials with mass production in mind? Will its price–value relationship turn a profit? How many ways can this product outperform the competition? How will the product be distributed? Will the product idea be licensed or will the inventor start a new business? Is it a stand-alone product or is it part of a product line? Does the product idea actually work in the real world? A good design process looks at the product and its potential from all angles.

Once the project is determined to be feasible, which may be as early as the research phase or as late as the end of the design phase, the planning and execution of a project plan begins. With the individual inventor, a project plan may be as basic as a notebook filled with notes, ideas, sketches, and statistics. With a large project in a corporation, it will be managed with project management software complete with phases, deadlines, and deliverables plus a full marketing plan. Project management software helps the project manager keep track of all phases of the process and tracks progress against deadlines.

Missed deadlines may indicate a bigger problem in product development—requirements creep. If the research and design phase was incomplete when the project began, often new requirements will crop up and will have to be addressed in the middle of the product's development. This can be a costly process in terms of time, money, and other resources. For example, when a product is seasonal and misses its production schedule, then the product is unlikely to achieve its greatest potential. Colored sunscreen is an example. Although it was intended for both summer fun outdoors

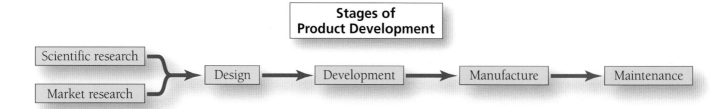

Stages of Product Development

Scientific research / Market research → Design → Development → Manufacture → Maintenance

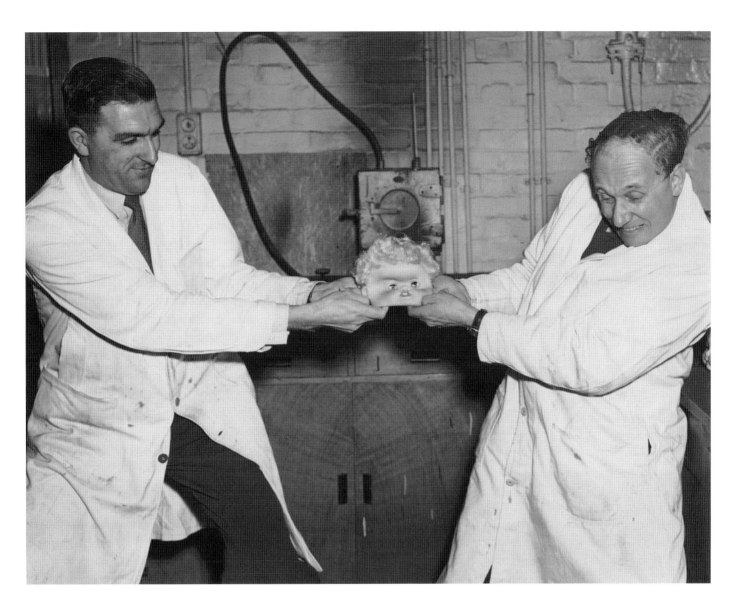

In 1953 two product testers check the durability of a doll's head.

and for winter skiing, the product was released late and missed its first window of opportunity.

Going from the design phase into production is more than a simple progression from the drawing board to the manufacturing plant. Manufacturing, distribution, and marketing all must be addressed simultaneously. Marketing and distribution are closely aligned—marketing makes the public aware of the product and distribution gets it to the right place at the right time. If the product is not shipped immediately upon completion through distribution channels, then the manufacturer must pay to store it. The ideal is to have the marketing campaign in place during manufacture, with distribution channels established before the product is completed.

Once a product is delivered to the consumer, another step in the product development process, depending on the product, may come into play. Some products provide warranties or require ongoing maintenance. Warranties can originate with the manufacturer or can be offered by wholesalers or distributors. Full-function wholesalers and distributors actually purchase the product from the manufacturer, and then resell it with a standard markup. In that case, the wholesaler or distributor may offer a warranty through its own stores. Other products, for example, appliances or electronics, may require maintenance. Even though the manufacturer does not typically service these products, the product development plan must include a plan for servicing those items.

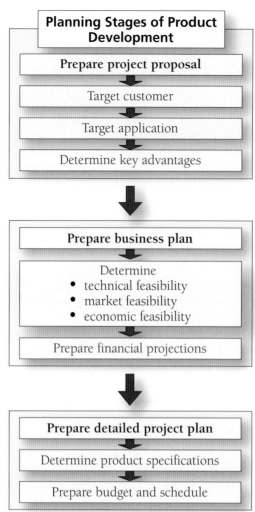

Planning Stages of Product Development

Prepare project proposal

Target customer

Target application

Determine key advantages

Prepare business plan

Determine
- technical feasibility
- market feasibility
- economic feasibility

Prepare financial projections

Prepare detailed project plan

Determine product specifications

Prepare budget and schedule

Source: Preston G. Smith and Donald G. Reinersten, *Developing New Products in Half the Time,* New York, Wiley, 1998.

Entrepreneurs

Entrepreneurial inventors face different issues than do big corporations in product development. First, they must have an idea that comes across as a sure winner right from the start. Unless inventors have enough money to manufacture, distribute, and market their products, they have to rely on other kinds of funding.

Family members might invest in a product without fully believing in the product if they believe in the inventor. However, most other investors require a convincing product and marketing plan before they will put up any money. A good idea is a good idea only if it works and if someone is willing to pay for it—both in the production phase and in the marketplace.

When individual inventors have ideas that they can make into salable products,

they must decide either to create a business to produce and sell that product or to license that product to another company to make and sell for them. Licensing the product and letting someone else manufacture, market, and distribute it may seem easier. However, most companies are not willing to purchase a license unless they are quite sure the product will be successful. If a large company will buy the license and put its marketing and distribution power behind the product, that can be very helpful to the individual inventor.

If the inventor tries to set up his or her own business, then the product must meet a few basic criteria. First, it must have some significant advantage over the competition. Second, that advantage must be easily shown or demonstrated on the packaging, particularly if little money is available for advertising. For example, an individual invents a power tool for woodworking that requires both precise handling and lots of instruction. Without a major advertising campaign to explain the tool's value to consumers, the tool will probably fail. Most consumers scan store shelves for purchases. If the product's value is not obvious on the package or from advertising, then consumers are unlikely to purchase.

Protecting an Idea

A patent is the most common method of protecting a scientific discovery or an idea for a new invention or improvement to an existing one. Although a patent offers some protection against those who would copy or steal the idea, it is not always the best route to take. The U.S. Patent Office works under an exchange system. The Patent Office grants exclusive use of a patented product or process for 20 years. In exchange, the content of the patent is put into a public repository where anyone can view it. The risk is that someone will take a patented idea and make changes or improvements. With enough change to the original idea, that person can then patent the new idea.

In some cases, a patent is not appropriate. For example, Kentucky Fried Chicken has not patented its "12 secret herbs and spices" because it wants to keep the recipe a secret. Instead, it works under a trade secret agreement where manufacturers of the spice mix agree not to reveal the recipe.

Trademarks can become a form of idea protection. If a certain product is associated with a particular name, consumers will lean toward that brand, protecting it from theft. For example, RollerBlades are a trademarked product (the generic name is inline skates). The same is true of Kleenex.

Collaboration

The individual inventor is not completely extinct, but the individual is being replaced by collaborative teams who work together to bring products to market. Increased competition makes every day count in the consumer market. Product cycle times are decreasing with advances in technology and business processes. Cheap labor in some parts of the world puts intense pressure on U.S. companies to find lower-cost methods of producing competing products. Lightning-speed advances in technology make it difficult for one company or product development team to keep up with all the changes. Accordingly, companies are beginning to collaborate on product development.

A large, multinational corporation may have engineers and designers in the United States, manufacturers in Taiwan, and marketing professionals worldwide working together to bring a product, for example, computer disk drives, to market. This kind of development effort requires focused project management and well-defined communication channels and structures. On a smaller scale, collaboration may be necessary among a company's scientists, engineers, marketers, managers, suppliers, sales force, and retailers; pharmaceuticals are an example.

Software product development becomes a major collaborative effort when working on a product like an enterprise information base that can be accessed through the

Software Development Cycles

Software development differs slightly from other product development. The manufacturing process is actually the coding process. The manufacturing cost of developing software lies in the expertise, labor, and computers that develop it and test it. Parts are not purchased, and the majority of actual product production costs are concentrated in the cost of documentation and disks or CDs. In the case of downloadable software, even those costs are eliminated.

The software development cycle includes the research phase, which is broken down into planning, then analysis. Both product and software development have a design phase, then a construction phase (called the development phase in product development). The implementation phase in software development is simply product distribution.

The maintenance phase is completely different in software development. Almost all software requires some kind of maintenance in the form of upgrades. Even if the product itself never changes in function, it must be updated to keep up with new technology or it will be relegated to the growing pile of obsolete software. Software also requires maintenance in the form of fixes (called patches) to correct any problems inherent in the software or with its compatibility with other products.

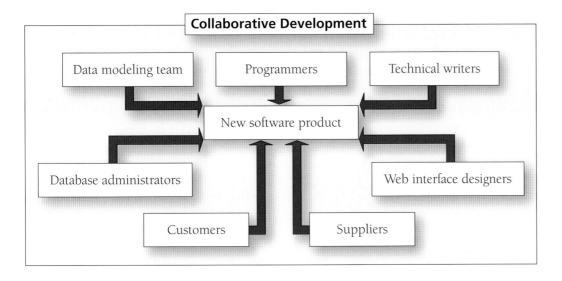

The collaborative development process for a new software product involves many different participants.

In a graphics studio, designers work on packaging for a new product.

Internet. Some of the technical professionals involved in such an effort are the data modeling team to design the database, the programmers to write the code, technical writers to document the system and create online help, Web interface designers, network engineers, and the database administrators who maintain the information stored in the database. Nontechnical individuals involved might be customers and suppliers who will use the database and their contacts inside the company. All of these teams must work together to bring a major software product to market.

Whenever the idea for a new or improved product begins—with an individual inventor working in a basement or a team of scientists working in a sophisticated lab—product development requires time, talent, and financial backing. The foundation of a successful product is thorough research coupled with a useful product idea. Developing that idea into a marketable product requires understanding what people want, determining the price–value relationship, and making the public aware that the product is available and that it is better than anything else they have access to today.

Further Reading

Crawford, Merle C., and C. Anthony Di Benedetto. *New Product Management*. 2nd ed. New York: McGraw-Hill, 1999.

Debelak, Don. *Entrepreneur Magazine Bringing Your Product to Market*. New York: John Wiley & Sons, 1997.

Gorchels, Linda. *The Product Manager's Handbook: The Complete Product Management Resource Guide*. New York: McGraw-Hill, 2000.

Hall, John A. *Bringing New Products to Market: The Art and Science of Creating Winners*. New York: AMACOM, 1991.

Husch, Tony, and Linda Foust. *That's a Great Idea! The New Product Handbook*. Oakland, Calif.: Gravity Publishing, 1986.

—*Stephanie Buckwalter*

Productivity

Productivity equals the quantity of goods and services produced by each hour of work. The level of productivity in an economy significantly affects how much its workers earn and how well its people live. Workers in countries like the United States and Germany produce more for each hour they work than do workers in Mexico or Pakistan; U.S. and German workers are paid more in great part because they are more productive. Productivity growth is the result of making more goods and services without putting in more hours of work. Productivity growth is the wellspring of prosperity and is the reason people today have more and better goods than their grandparents had without working more hours.

Why Productivity Matters

Over time, an economy's growth rate equals the growth of its labor force (the increase in the number of people available for work) plus the growth in its productivity (the amount each worker produces). "Productivity isn't everything, but in the long run, it's almost everything," Paul Krugman, the Princeton University economist and *New York Times* columnist, has written. Average wages grow in line with productivity growth. Most people get most of their income from wages. Thus, as productivity increases, economic progress from one generation to the next increases also.

Productivity in the United States grew very rapidly (about 2.9 percent annually) in the 25 years following the end of World War II. Around 1973 productivity growth slowed mysteriously to about 1.3 percent annually. Economists still argue about the reasons for the falloff. Whatever the cause, slow productivity growth hurt wages and economic progress thereafter for more than two decades, producing an era that Krugman once called "the age of diminished expectations."

This slow growth in productivity was particularly disappointing and puzzling because it coincided with the computer revolution; this phenomenon came to be known as the productivity paradox. "You can see the computer age everywhere but in the productivity statistics," Robert Solow, a Nobel Prize–winning economist at the Massachusetts Institute of Technology, observed in 1987. A surprisingly long time is often needed for a nation and its economy to determine how to harness a new technology. In the early part of the twentieth century, about two decades passed while businesses figured out how to get the most out of electricity, the new technology of that era. Only then did electricity yield an increase in productivity.

U.S. productivity quickened again around 1995, growing at an annual rate of 2.5 percent between 1995 and 2000. This surge in productivity was the essence of what was known as the New Economy, showing, according to most economic observers, that computers, communications technology, and the Internet were finally being used efficiently.

At the beginning of the twenty-first century, as the United States began recovering from recession, the question of the strength of the productivity boom of the late 1990s remained unanswered. Few economists expected productivity to match the remarkable pace of the late 1990s, but few expected it to return to the dismal pace of the 1970s and 1980s. Seemingly small changes in the rate of productivity growth can have a great effect. A sustained half-percentage point rise in productivity results in the federal government collecting $1.2 trillion more from taxpayers over 10 years; a faster-growing economy also engenders more income and more profits.

See also:
Capital; Gross Domestic Product; Human Capital; Industrial Revolution; Information Revolution; Information Technology; Innovation.

U.S. Productivity Eras	
Annual growth in U.S. productivity, or output per hour of work.	
1947 to 1973	2.9%
1973 to 1995	1.3%
1995 to 2000	2.5%

Note: The annual growth in U.S. productivity, measured as output per hour of work.
Source: Bureau of Labor Statistics, http://www.bls.gov/lpc/iprdata1.htm (March 13, 2003).

Productivity in the United States grew rapidly for the quarter-century after World War II, slowed mysteriously around 1973, and then rose again around 1995.

Even workers who are not more productive themselves benefit when productivity grows. The typical barber, for instance, does not cut any more heads of hair in an hour today than barbers did 50 years ago. Yet barbers make more money today than they did 50 years ago. Why? Because rising productivity elsewhere in the economy has pushed up other workers' wages. If barbers today earned what barbers earned 50 years ago, no one would cut hair for a living. Barbers' wages have risen with everyone else's.

Why Productivity Growth Changes

What causes changes in the amount of output produced for each hour of work? Productivity growth often slows during recessions, or periods of reduced economic activity, and increases afterward, when businesses expand production rapidly without adding many new workers. The changes in productivity that matter, however, are best measured over long periods. Workers' productivity can be improved by equipping them with more and better machines that allow them to produce more in a normal workday. Another method is to invent a whole new way of doing something. Sending messages by e-mail instead of postal mail, for instance, can accomplish the same task with fewer hours of work; the Internet has no mail clerks or mail carriers. New techniques for organizing the workplace—for example, the assembly line in the early part of the twentieth century and self-managed work teams in the late twentieth century—can yield the same output with fewer workers and thus increase productivity. Training workers can also make them more efficient and thus more productive.

An automated Toyota assembly line in Miyazaki, Japan. Productivity has been improved through the incorporation of robotic equipment.

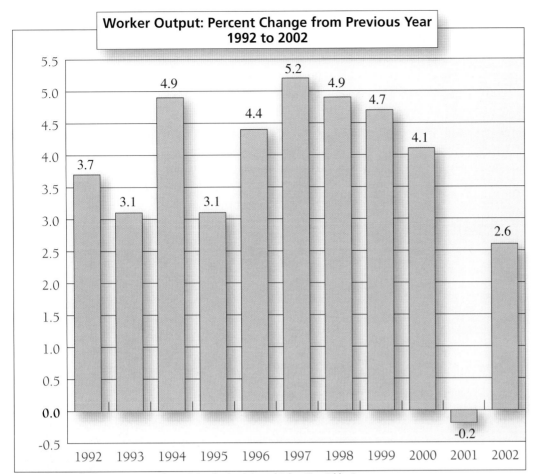

Worker Output: Percent Change from Previous Year 1992 to 2002

Year	Percent Change
1992	3.7
1993	3.1
1994	4.9
1995	3.1
1996	4.4
1997	5.2
1998	4.9
1999	4.7
2000	4.1
2001	-0.2
2002	2.6

Source: Bureau of Labor Statistics, "Industry Labor Productivity and Labor Cost Tables," http://www.bls.gov/lpc/iprdata1.htm (April 3, 2003).

Most economists believe that spending more on research and development, investing more in new technologies, and improving the education of the population are the best ways for a society to try to increase the pace of productivity growth. Reorganizing an economy so that it uses resources more efficiently can also increase productivity. In the United States, the deregulation of important industries like trucking and airlines probably boosted productivity because it forced companies to compete with one another and find better ways of operating. Competition from imported goods accomplishes much the same goal by keeping U.S. producers under constant pressure to improve productivity. Information technology and reduced regulation helps lessen the friction in the economy—the time wasted on nonproductive tasks like filling out forms or counting parts—and, thus, helps increase productivity.

Why Productivity Sometimes Has a Bad Reputation

Productivity is sometimes blamed for layoffs. If Ford Motor Company can produce more cars with fewer workers, it will employ fewer people. For the individual worker, losing a job may be catastrophic, but for the economy as a whole, an increase in productivity is a benefit. A particular company or an entire industry may shrink, but, in a growing economy, other companies and industries spring up to employ people.

Agriculture is an example. In 1800 an American farmer needed 344 hours to produce 100 bushels of corn. A century later, a farmer needed 147 hours. By 1980 those 100 bushels took three hours of work. Richer land was farmed; better machinery and pesticides were used; labor-saving techniques were perfected. Many fewer workers were required to feed the American population. In 1800, 75 percent of all American

Although computers became ubiquitous in U.S. offices in the 1980s, about 15 years were to pass before their effect was felt in productivity growth.

workers were farmers. By 1900 only 40 percent were. Only 3 percent of Americans now work on farms. The change was tough on nineteenth-century farm families, many of whom were forced off their farms or unable to employ their children. It destroyed some farm towns and a way of life. However, Americans overall are better off. They eat as much as or more than their grandparents did, but they spend much less time growing food, so they are freed to engage in other occupations—direct movies, teach math, read X rays, and give massages, for example. Although many fewer Americans work on farms, the country has food to spare, which can be traded with other nations for oil and other goods. The same process is happening to factories. They employ a shrinking fraction of American workers, but they produce more goods. Yet the U.S. economy continues to create more jobs almost every year.

Productivity grew rapidly in the last half of the 1990s, but the unemployment rate was lower than it had been in decades.

Some argue that information technology is different—that it will destroy jobs faster than new ones can be created. "Factory workers, secretaries, receptionists, clerical workers, salesclerks, bank tellers, telephone operators, librarians, wholesalers and middle managers are just a few of the many occupations destined for virtual elimination," warns author Jeremy Rifkin. "In the United States alone, as many as 90 million jobs in a labor force of 124 million are vulnerable to displacement by automation." Nearly all economists reject this view. Nonetheless, productivity growth does not guarantee that the benefits will be shared evenly. It pushes up the average wage, but wages for some workers may rise and wages for other workers may fall.

Why Measuring Productivity Is Difficult

Productivity, like nearly everything in a modern economy, is usually gauged by the monetary value of a worker's output because comparing, say, tons of steel with numbers of heart transplants is very difficult. The market generally values what a heart surgeon can do in one hour more than it values the service that a waitress provides in an hour, so the heart surgeon is considered more productive.

Calculating productivity is easy in principle, hard in practice. The numbers published by the government are, at best, a good approximation of reality. Calculating the productivity of steelworkers is relatively simple. Steel companies can provide the government with the number of tons of steel each mill produces in a year and the number of hours the workers put in. The government divides the two to get a measure of tons of steel per hour of work. By comparing one year's figures with those of the next, the government calculates growth in productivity in the steel industry.

Measuring the output of high school teachers is much harder. Should it be measured by the number of students they teach? Or how much the students learn? Measuring the productivity of public health nurses, business consultants, television anchors, software writers, and many of the other people who work in service, rather than manufacturing, is similarly difficult.

Industries in which the product—personal computers, for example—keeps getting better also present difficulties in measuring productivity. The same number of hours may be required to design and build a computer as last year, but as this year's computer is much faster and smarter, the workers' output has increased—and thus their productivity has risen. The government tries to adjust for changes in the quality of the goods and services produced, but the precise adjustment is hard to make. The U.S. Labor Department's Bureau of Labor Statistics posts the latest productivity statistics and historical data on its Web site (http://www.bls.gov/lpc/home.htm).

Comparing productivity among countries is difficult, and different measures yield different results. By most measures, workers in the United States are the most productive in the world. Figures for Germany include both the very productive workers in what was once West Germany and the less productive workers in what was East Germany.

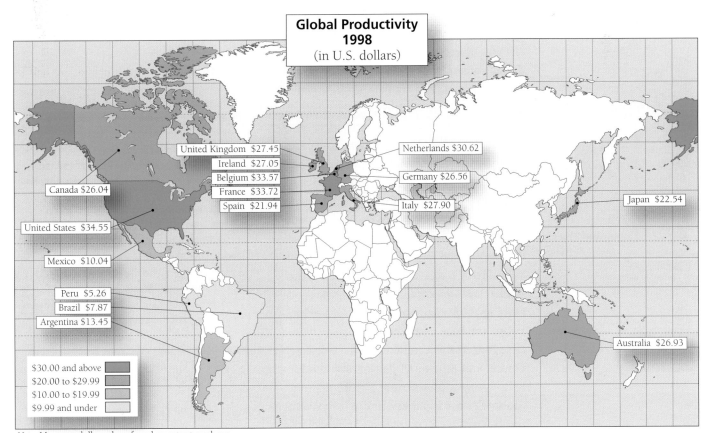

Global Productivity 1998
(in U.S. dollars)

United Kingdom $27.45
Ireland $27.05
Belgium $33.57
France $33.72
Spain $21.94
Canada $26.04
United States $34.55
Mexico $10.04
Peru $5.26
Brazil $7.87
Argentina $13.45
Netherlands $30.62
Germany $26.56
Italy $27.90
Japan $22.54
Australia $26.93

$30.00 and above
$20.00 to $29.99
$10.00 to $19.99
$9.99 and under

Note: Measures dollar value of worker output per hour.
Source: *The World Economy: A Millennial Perspective*, Paris, Organization for Economic Cooperation and Development, 2001.

How should the productivity of this computer science teacher be measured? By the number of students he teaches, by the amount his students learn, or by some other measure?

Comparing productivity levels among countries is complicated by differences in the ways economies are measured, by changes in currency exchange rates, and by disagreements among economists about the most meaningful way to compare economies that differ markedly in the percentage of adults in the workforce. Most widely used measures rank U.S. workers as the most productive in the world. Economists generally expect the gap between U.S. workers and those in other countries to narrow as other economies learn from the United States and begin to use similar technologies. One of the big economic puzzles is the question: Why did the forces of the New Economy that yielded such an impressive surge in productivity in the United States in the late 1990s fail to produce a similar increase in other large, successful economies, like Germany, France, and Britain? Understanding productivity—why it grows more quickly in some countries than in others, and what governments, employers, unions, and colleges and high schools can do to spur its growth—

remains an area of research in economics that bears directly on the well-being of future generations.

Further Reading

Bauer, Paul W., Jeffrey L. Jensen, and Mark E. Schweizer. "Productivity Gains: How Permanent?" Economic Commentary, Sept. 1, 2001. http://www.clev.frb.org/research/com2001/0901.htm (March 13, 2002).

Blinder, Alan. "Policy Brief: The Internet and the New Economy." The Brookings Institution, June 2000. http://www.brook.edu/comm/policy-briefs/pb060/pb60.htm (March 13, 2003).

Davis, Bob, and David Wessel. *Prosperity: The Coming 20-Year Boom and What It Means to You.* New York: Times Business, 1998.

DeLong, J. Bradford. "Do We Have a 'New' Macroeconomy?" March 2001. http://www.j-bradford-delong.net/Econ_Articles/Jaffe/new_macroeconomy.html (March 13, 2003).

Gordon, Robert J. "Does the 'New Economy' Measure Up to the Great Inventions of the Past?" *Journal of Economic Perspectives* 14 (Fall 2000): 49.

Rifkin, Jeremy. *The End of Work.* New York: G. P. Putnam's Sons, 1995.

—*David Wessel*

Product Liability

See also:
Business Law; Liability;
Regulation of Business and
Industry.

Product liability is the responsibility a manufacturer or seller incurs when a person or a group has been injured by its product, typically due to a defect in the product's design or manufacture. Product liability law (torts) is constantly subject to analysis, debate, and reform.

In a product liability lawsuit, a case may be based on the principle of negligence, which requires the plaintiff to prove that the injury-producing defect resulted from a specific act of negligence (failure to take reasonable care) by the manufacturer or seller. For instance, lawsuits related to the spate of Ford Explorer accidents in the 1990s claimed that Bridgestone/Firestone, the manufacturer of the tires Ford used, was negligent in the design and manufacture of the tire and that Ford was negligent in the design of the car.

American tort law underwent a transformation in the 1960s, when most states, wishing to provide more comprehensive consumer protection against harmful products, adopted the principle of strict liability in addition to negligence. In strict liability cases, liability is incurred even if a manufacturer or seller exercised all possible care in the preparation and sale of the product. Strict liability focuses on the product, not on the conduct of the manufacturer or seller. The plaintiff must establish only that the product was sold in a condition that was unreasonably dangerous to the consumer. Under strict liability principles, every party involved in the chain of distribution may be found liable, including suppliers of components and raw materials, assembling manufacturers, wholesalers, and retailers.

If a company is found liable for injury, its responsibility usually translates to a monetary sum, or damages, it is required to pay the injured party. Compensatory damages for personal injury include current and future medical and hospital expenses, loss of earnings, and pain and suffering. Punitive damages, as the name suggests, are designed to punish the company for distributing a defective or dangerous product.

How Can Companies Limit Their Liability?
While in the best-case scenario, companies invest time and money in product safety research, high-quality materials, and safe manufacturing processes, not all products can be made perfectly reliable or harmless. Prudent companies maintain product liability insurance and take steps to protect themselves against exposure to liability claims.

A Firestone tire on a wrecked Ford Explorer that is to be used as evidence in a lawsuit against Ford Motor Company and Bridgestone/Firestone, Inc., in 2001.

They provide clear instructions for the safe use of their product, disclaimers of liability, and provisions in their warranties and contracts that explicitly state for what use their product is and is not intended.

Even warning labels can offer manufacturers a degree of protection. Warning labels are common, cautioning against using a hair dryer near water, keeping a car running while filling the gas tank, or placing hands or feet near the blades of lawnmowers or chainsaws. Some of these warnings may seem obvious; however, companies are prudent to include them and may be able to limit their liability by providing clear and well-placed statements related to the proper use of their products.

Our legal system, however, ensures that no manufacturer or seller can completely absolve itself of liability through such statements. Courts have the final say in determining if a manufacturer or seller is liable for an injury.

To Sue or Not to Sue

Critics of the U.S. justice system argue that too often product liability cases hold companies responsible for what is, in fact, consumer negligence. One case that sparked such controversy was Stella Liebeck's 1994 suit against McDonald's: a jury awarded her nearly $2.9 million in punitive damages after she suffered third-degree burns in spilling McDonald's coffee onto her lap. Although a judge later reduced the punitive award to $480,000, many still wondered why McDonald's should be held in any way responsible for Liebeck's accident. Indeed, a *Seinfeld* episode later satirized the notion that a coffee retailer would be liable for such an injury, reflecting the public attitude toward Liebeck's seemingly outrageous claim against McDonald's.

Some critics are similarly puzzled by the recent flurry of suits against tobacco companies. In the 1990s and on into the twenty-first century, individuals, state and federal governments, and even the governments of other countries have filed suit against U.S. tobacco companies like Philip Morris and R. J. Reynolds, charging them with liability for smoking-related health problems. Several tobacco companies are so burdened by litigation that they are threatened with bankruptcy. A common argument against such lawsuits is that people have known about the harmful effects of smoking since 1964, when the U.S. surgeon general first issued a tobacco warning. Another common argument is that the federal government should itself be included in such suits, for its history of support of tobacco companies. Both the McDonald's and tobacco company cases reveal a kind of haziness in product liability law: Where does the manufacturer's responsibility end and the consumers' and governments' begin?

Answering this question in universal terms is difficult. Examining the details of each suit is necessary. For instance, in Liebeck's suit against McDonald's, the jury based its decision on the fact that McDonald's sells coffee at far higher temperatures than most other coffee retailers. The court determined that McDonald's was fully aware of the hazards of these high temperatures, as evidenced by hundreds of similar complaints in the past. Successful suits against tobacco companies have shown that the companies concealed research that indicated the harmful effects of nicotine and tobacco.

Without the liability lawsuits that brought such revelations to light, the public might never have become aware of these products' degree of dangerousness. Proponents of such litigation further argue that because so many companies have been forced to create safer products, factories and plants have reduced the risks their machines pose to workers, harmful medical products and toys have been removed from the market, and toxic materials like lead and asbestos have been eliminated from paints and buildings.

These kinds of positive changes do not apply only to the companies involved in litigation. Liability lawsuits often directly result in new state and federal laws that affect all manufacturers of related products. Even more effective is the fear that such lawsuits create.

Chocolate products are displayed in a Los Angeles courtroom in 2002 during a lawsuit against major chocolate manufacturers, including Nestlé, Kraft, and Hershey's. The lawsuit alleges chocolate contains lead and cadmium and seeks warning labels alerting consumers to any potential danger.

All companies become motivated to redesign or further research the safety of their products, provide clearer instructions and terms of use, include better warning labels on their products, and in general reduce the risks they pose to health and the environment.

The legal system does have the responsibility, however, to guard against lawyers who bring frivolous liability lawsuits that prey on the innocent and guilty alike, or who take advantage of an alarmed and angry public to secure jury awards that far exceed a justifiable amount. Such tactics are not only unfair, but may also create serious problems. Companies reluctant to assume liability risks or pay the high costs of liability insurance may simply withdraw their products from the market—products that may be essential to public health or economic well-being.

For example, suppliers of raw materials to medical device manufacturers have withdrawn from the market, daunted by the high cost of legal defenses for product liability lawsuits. This has, in turn, forced a sharp increase in the price of medical devices, affecting consumers whom liability laws are designed to protect. Supporters of tort reform argue that laws should set limits on the damages that may be awarded, create penalties for frivolous lawsuits, and generally encourage personal responsibility for the careful use of a product.

Many critics share the concern that a legal system clogged by endless lawsuits creates a lack of faith in the system altogether. The United States has an average of 70,000 product liability lawsuits brought each year, vastly more than in other countries. At the same time, any new legislation must take care not to erase more than 30 years of reform that has increasingly put the consumer first, rather than big businesses with lobbying power. Perhaps President Bill Clinton said it best in remarks regarding his veto of a 1996 product liability bill: "It is a hallmark of our system of justice that when a product produces injury or death a family has the right to try and recover its losses . . . . Any legal reform must be carefully crafted so that the interest of consumers and businesses are fairly balanced."

Further Reading

Cornwell, John. *The Power to Harm: Mind, Medicine and Murder on Trial.* New York: Viking Press, 1996.

Drivon, Laurence E., with Bob Schmidt. *The Civil War on Consumer Rights.* Berkeley, Calif.: Conari Press, 1990.

Huber, Peter W. *Liability: The Legal Revolution and Its Consequences.* New York: Basic Books, 1988.

Orey, Michael. *Assuming the Risk: The Mavericks, the Lawyers and the Whistle-Blowers Who Beat Big Tobacco.* Boston: Little, Brown, 1999.

—*Andrea Troyer and John Troyer*

See also:
Chambers of Commerce

Professional Associations

Professional associations are organizations that serve the interests of their members. They are usually nonprofit entities and are sometimes referred to as professional societies, trade associations, or professional organizations. Whatever name they use, they exist to provide a wide range of services for their members.

The main objective of professional associations is to expand the knowledge and skills of their members while helping them to meet and maintain a set of professional standards. For example, the American Medical Association (AMA) strives to serve as the voice of the American medical profession, serving more than 650,000 doctors in the United States. Founded more than 150 years ago, AMA's strategic agenda remains rooted in its historic commitment to standards, ethics, excellence in medical education and practice, and advocacy on behalf of the medical profession and the patients it serves. The AMA's work includes the development and promotion of standards in medical practice, research, and education; advocacy on behalf of patients and physicians; and the commitment to providing timely information on matters important to health.

Another example of a professional association is the National Association of Elementary School Principals (NAESP), which was founded in 1921 by a group of principals who sought to promote their profession and to provide a national forum for their ideas. The NAESP promotes professional standards and provides a peer network of more than 28,500 principals worldwide.

Some professional associations are large organizations with big budgets, while others are much smaller. All professional associations stand ready to serve their members in a variety of ways. For example, the Credit Union National Association (CUNA), based in Washington, D.C., and Madison, Wisconsin, is the premier national trade association serving America's credit unions. CUNA provides many services to credit unions, including representation, information, public relations, continuing professional education, and business development. CUNA also works with related organizations to provide products and services to credit unions.

Not all professional associations are organized by trade. For example, the Financial Women's Association (FWA) was founded in 1956 to help shape leaders in business and finance with a special emphasis on the role and development of women. The FWA serves its members through educational programs and networking opportunities and serves the community through scholarships, mentoring, and training programs.

Professional associations do share some common services. For example, most will provide public relations information to both local and national media, as well as collect and publish statistics on their specific industry. They also sponsor regional and national

---

5 Largest U.S. Professional Associations

- National Association of Realtors
- American Bar Association
- American Institute of Certified Public Accountants
- American Medical Association
- Institute of Electrical and Electronic Engineers

---

5 Largest U.S. Professional Trade Associations

- U.S. Chamber of Commerce
- National Association of Home Builders
- American Management Association
- U.S. Hispanic Chamber of Commerce
- American Library Association

One of the roles of professional associations is to organize trade shows; SIGGRAPH, a convention of computer graphics professionals, is organized by the Association for Computing Machinery.

conferences, provide continuing education services for their members, and advise members on a wide range of management issues and policies. Some, but not all, professional agencies have a government relations department in which they monitor government activities concerning their industry. Just about every professional association has its own Web site that helps it stay in communication with members.

Most professional associations offer either an electronic newsletter or magazine, or a print publication, which is distributed to their members. Many times professional associations will compile and publish information that is available only to their members. Sales data that are of interest to sales professionals, or research and statistical surveys, would be examples.

Professional associations also sponsor trade shows. For example, the National Association of Independent Schools (NAIS) sponsors an annual conference along with a trade show. It is held in a different city each year and it attracts more than 5,000 educators. During its annual event, NAIS offers a wide variety of educational workshops, plenary sessions, and an exhibit hall with vendors. Such a gathering permits members to learn what is new in their industry, network with other professionals in their field, visit a new vendor, and perhaps even check out new employment opportunities.

Each professional association is free to impose membership requirements, develop mission statements, and set goals. Associations have a governing body composed of members in their industry. Some associations have nominal membership fees, others cost thousands of dollars per year to join.

Many industries have several professional associations that serve that industry, both on the national and local level. For example, the fund raising industry has a national organization, the National Society of Fund Raising Executives, while fund raising professionals in the state of Delaware can also join the Delaware Association of Nonprofit Agencies. Most professional associations help promote the different industries they represent, and each year new organizations are created. The *Encyclopedia of Associations* lists nearly all of the professional associations in the United States.

Further Reading:

American Society of Association Executives, Gateway to Associations. http://www.asaenet.org (March 13, 2003).

Sheets, Tara, ed. *Encyclopedia of Associations.* Detroit, Mich.: Gale Group, 2001.

—John Riddle

See also:

Capitalism; Competition; Regulation of Business and Industry; Supply and Demand.

Profit and Loss

The fundamental lure of capitalism is based on its assessment of human nature. Its central idea is that greed is the most powerful motivator for behavior. People naturally want to profit, or gain economic resources, through their activities. In addition, they will also act to avoid losses. These motives create simple and powerful reinforcement of each other. Economic activities that create profits are rewarded because free enterprise emphasizes the protection of private property, which allows individuals to keep their profits and use them as they see fit. Publicly traded corporations either pay profits to owners in the form of dividends or reinvest the money to increase the value of the company. Unprofitable decisions (and bad luck) are punished by losses, which make individuals and businesses worse off by increasing their debts or reducing the value of their assets.

The concepts of profit and loss are distinct to capitalism. Indeed, precapitalist enterprises did not concern themselves with profit and loss; costs were not of particular interest to merchants in the eighteenth century, for example. With the rise of big business in the nineteenth century, however, costs became much more important; a firm that lowers its costs can increase its profits and outsell its competition. For instance, steel magnate Andrew Carnegie ruthlessly lowered costs to gain market share. Others sold goods at prices below cost—that is, at a loss—to drive out competitors. John Rockefeller did this at times with his Standard Oil Company; in the late twentieth century, Japan used the same technique to expand its steel industry.

Supply and Demand

The free enterprise system uses prices to reflect the value of goods and services. In brief, prices are set by the combination of supply and demand. Supply is the number of products or services producers will make at a certain price. Demand is the number of products or services consumers will use at a certain price. Goods in short supply or that are in high demand have high prices and provide strong profit opportunities; the opposite also holds true.

Creating a profit requires producers to anticipate consumer demand and to manage efficiently how they supply goods and services. Both are inexact sciences because they rely on events in the future that can be hard to predict.

Demand for a product is driven by several factors, including the availability of substitutes, the incomes of consumers, changes in the weather, and a host of other variables. Part of the challenge of running a business is that most of these elements are essentially outside the control of the business. As demand can change at any time, so can prices and therefore profits. For example, good weather may erode the profits of an umbrella manufacturer however well the business is run.

Demand is closely connected to the strength of the economy and consumer confidence. When the economy is expanding, jobs are usually plentiful and incomes are usually rising, leading to higher profits. Conversely, when the economy is weak, many businesses cut back production and may experience losses until demand begins to grow again.

Businesses also face risk in the supply side of the equation. Supply will change with the costs of production, the number of sellers, and the expectations of consumers. Changes in any of these can affect supply and therefore prices and profits.

Businesses have developed a number of tools to help manage both the demand and

The Functions of Profit

- Serves as signal for allocating resources
- Serves as incentive for innovation and risk taking
- Rewards efficiency

Source: Dewin Mansfield and Nariman Behrauesh, *Economics USA*, 5th ed., New York, Norton, 1998.

supply factors involved in profit and loss. The most widespread tool for managing demand is the use of marketing, or advertising. The purpose of marketing is to interest consumers in a good or service. Effective ads accomplish two objectives: (1) directly increase sales and (2) build brand loyalty, or the habit in consumers of using the advertiser's product or service. Both are intended to increase profitability.

The supply portion of the equation is far easier for businesses to address as it depends on the choices that businesses make. Businesses invest a tremendous amount of time and energy in increasing their labor productivity and improving their management techniques. Labor productivity is the amount that workers can produce in a given amount of time. Increasing productivity allows employees to produce more and better products in the same amount of time and therefore create labor savings. Companies can invest in human resources or capital resources to increase their productivity. Human resources entail upgrading the education and skills of the workers; capital resources involve purchasing updated production equipment. Both result in lower costs and increased profits.

Profit and Loss, Competition, and the Government

Governments play an important role in the profitability of business. Total government spending in many countries is very high, and businesses that gain contracts with government agencies have a profit opportunity. Governments also control taxation, property rights, and regulation, all of which affect businesses. Regulations are laws established to limit businesses and blunt the excesses of the free market. Examples include environmental laws and minimum wage requirements. Corporations often seek exemptions from regulation (or delay the implementation of regulations with lawsuits) and therefore increase their profits. Governments can also eliminate competition for a good or service by granting a producer monopoly status, allowing one

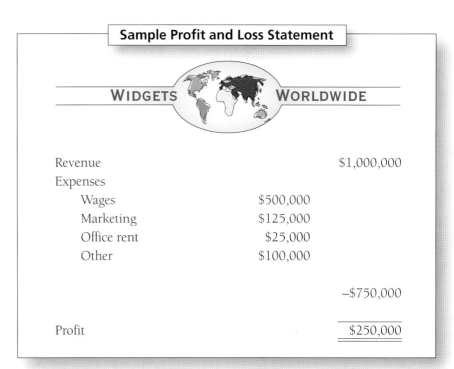

Sample Profit and Loss Statement

WIDGETS WORLDWIDE

Revenue		$1,000,000
Expenses		
Wages	$500,000	
Marketing	$125,000	
Office rent	$25,000	
Other	$100,000	
		−$750,000
Profit		$250,000

company the exclusive right to produce a product without competition.

Businesses commonly act to reduce competition without the aid of government. This was the preferred method of doing business for nineteenth-century tycoons, including John D. Rockefeller and J. P. Morgan. They created trusts in the steel, sugar, and other industries; these trusts coordinated prices and production to stabilize supply and maximize profits. Such arrangements eventually resulted in government action after public outcry over high prices. The Sherman Antitrust Act was passed in 1890, making illegal the creation of a monopoly or the coordination of actions by businesses to "restrain trade." Other measures soon followed that broke up the trusts and prevented new ones from being created.

The enforcement of these laws has led to some of the most prominent legal cases in American history. Microsoft Corporation was sued by the government for monopolizing the market for desktop operating software. The computer company settled with the government after years of litigation, agreeing to discontinue certain practices.

The lure of high profits gives businesses a strong incentive to continue attempts to limit competition. A common method is mergers and acquisitions—the act of buying competing companies. Mergers can provide several benefits to a corporation. One is the immediate reduction in competition. The combining companies' streamlined operations is another. For example, merging companies commonly lay off workers when the new company is more productive. Governments regulate mergers under antitrust law for the same reason that they restrict monopolies. Less competition often means higher prices for consumers.

Calculating and Reporting Profit and Loss

Calculating profit and loss has become more difficult as businesses grow larger and engage in more complex and varied operations. Exxon-Mobil is an example. It was the most profitable company in the world in 2001, earning more than $15 billion. It also employed tens of thousands of workers in dozens of countries across the world.

One result of the scale and complexity of modern business has been the growth of the field of accounting. Accountants are financial experts who usually have four-year college degrees. One function of accountancy is to keep track of the financial transactions of corporations. Many companies require financial experts because they employ thousands of workers and earn billions of dollars. The most important function of accountants is to ensure that the financial health of a company is accurately measured. Publicly traded firms are required to have outside accountants audit them, or examine their books. An annual report is published with the details of a company's assets and liabilities provided in a balance sheet.

A central feature of this report is its calculation of the company's annual profit or loss. As corporate finance has become so complex, accountants have developed standard procedures, general and accepted accounting practices, to allow the easy comparison of

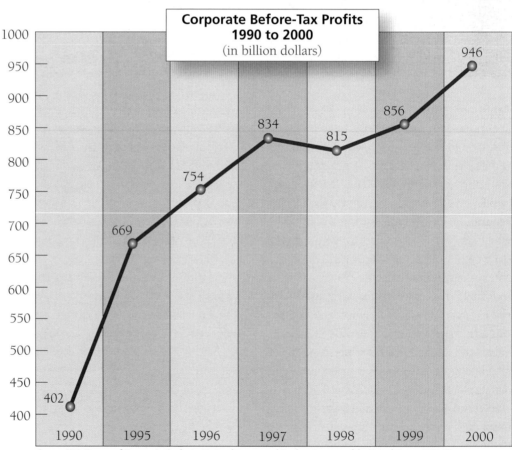

Corporate Before-Tax Profits 1990 to 2000
(in billion dollars)

Source: U.S. Bureau of Economic Analysis, *National Income and Product Accounts of the United States, 1929-97,* and *Survey of Current Business,* July 2001.

corporate results. The annual report also details how the company spent any profits or absorbed losses.

The monitoring process is very important in the economy. It is intended to ensure public trust that the information needed to accurately price stocks is freely available, which, in turn, encourages confidence in the stock market and increases the funding available for corporations.

The oversight process remains imperfect. For example, in 2001 the Enron Corporation was lionized as one of the world's most profitable and best run firms. By July 2002 it was forced to declare bankruptcy after news that management had disguised losses and generated fictitious profits through accounting fraud. The U.S. government reacted quickly to the scandal by increasing penalties for corporate malfeasance and pressing criminal charges against company officials. The reforms are designed to bolster investor confidence by ensuring that profits and losses are accurately reported.

An Exxon-Mobil fuel processing plant in Carson, California. In 2001 Exxon-Mobil was the most profitable company in the world.

Further Reading

Burrough, Bryan, and John Helyar. *Barbarians at the Gate: The Fall of RJR Nabisco.* New York: Harper Collins, 1991.

Fusaro, Peter, and Ross Miller. *What Went Wrong at Enron: Everyone's Guide to the Largest Bankruptcy in U.S. History.* Hoboken, N.J.: John Wiley and Sons, 2002.

Lewis, Michael. *Liar's Poker: Rising through the Wreckage on Wall Street.* New York: Penguin Books, 1990.

Peters, Thomas, and Robert Waterman. *In Search of Excellence: Lessons from America's Best-Run Companies.* New York: Warner Books, 1988.

Walton, Sam. *Made in America: My Story.* New York: Bantam Books, 1993.

—*David Long*

See also:
Balance of Trade; Tariff.

Protectionism

Economists generally agree that free trade is in the best interests of all countries. Free trade involves the ready movement of goods between countries, with every country having open access to other countries' markets. However, within many countries, some argue that free trade is harmful to either the country as a whole or certain groups within it. These groups will lobby their political representatives for a restriction on imports. In response, politicians can "protect" certain industries by limiting free trade by use of various protectionist measures. This protection does not come without costs.

Kinds of Protectionism

The most common ways to reduce imports into a country are by imposing tariffs and quotas. Tariffs are taxes placed on imported goods. Tariffs are of three kinds: ad valorem, specific, and compound. An ad valorem tariff is similar to a sales tax in that it is a percentage of the price of the product. A 10 percent ad valorem tariff imposes a 10 percent tax on the imported good. The tariff does generate revenue for a government. However, unlike a sales tax, governments rarely impose tariffs to raise revenues; tariff revenue in the United States accounts for only 1 percent of all government revenues.

A specific tariff involves a fixed amount of money per unit. For example, if Japanese carmakers were charged $100 for every car imported, that would be a specific tariff. Compound tariffs are a combination of ad valorem and specific tariffs. For example, in the United States imported wool blankets are faced with a 6 percent ad valorem tariff and a 1.8 cents-per-kilogram specific tariff.

Quotas involve a physical limit on the number of units of a particular product allowed to enter a country. The United States restricts the amount of cheese that can be imported with varying quotas that depend on the country exporting the cheese and the kind of cheese. For example, the United States allows only 1.85 million kilograms of Swiss cheese from Switzerland into the country. Other ways to restrict the amount of imports coming into a country exist; however, tariffs and quotas are the most used. Tariffs and quotas are sometimes imposed concurrently.

Effects of Protectionism

When trade restrictions are placed on imported products, the cost of those goods increases. In the case of the tariff, this tax will increase the price that consumers must pay. In the case of a quota, by reducing the amount of a good available in a country, the price of that product will rise. Local consumers will probably not buy as much. Protectionist measures harm local consumers as they must pay more for goods.

Tariffs and quotas do protect local jobs. Consumers will often turn to locally produced

Barriers to Trade		
Tariffs	**Quotas**	**Other**
• Ad valorem: percentage of price of product • Specific: fixed amount of money per unit • Compound: combination of ad valorem and specific tariffs	• Physical limit on number of units allowed into a country	• Prohibitions • Licensing schemes • Export restraint arrangements • Health and quarantine measures

Source: World Bank, "General Tariff Data," http://www.worldbank.org/data/wdi2001/pdfs/tab6_6.pdf (June 2, 2003).

products instead of the now relatively more expensive imported goods. As consumers buy less of the imported products and more of the local goods, local producers will increase their sales and hire more workers. Those who benefit from protection are the domestic producers of the goods and workers who are competing with imported products. When imports of cheese are restricted, U.S. cheese producers and workers in the cheese industry gain, but consumers pay a higher price for cheese than they would without the restrictions.

Debating Protectionism

A major rationale for protectionism is protection of local jobs. What typically occurs is that lower-priced imports are hurting local businesses, which then lay off their workers. With restrictions against the imported good in place, these local producers will be able to maintain their sales and employment levels. An argument heard often is that the low cost of labor in the exporting country is the basis for the low cost of imports.

However, many economists would say that low labor costs abroad are not a serious

In Switzerland two men move wheels of cheese with a forklift. The United States limits the amount of Swiss cheese that can be imported to protect domestic producers.

problem. The lower labor costs allow consumers to spend less for goods, saving them considerable money. Inexpensive foreign labor is often much less productive than are U.S. workers; as a result, the actual costs are not that much lower in the foreign countries. Even if they are, why not allow our consumers to buy from the country that can produce the best product at the lowest price?

Some argue that protectionist measures are necessary when other countries are engaged in unfair trade practices. These can include dumping (selling exported products below the cost of production) and foreign subsidies on production. Subsidies will lower a firm's production costs and therefore lower the price of the product on the international market. In such cases, the importing country may decide to place a tariff on the good to compensate for the production subsidy.

Tariffs were applied in the steel industry in the United States. The European Union, South Korea, and Brazil all heavily subsidize local steel industries. In March

2002 President George W. Bush announced a program, Steel Remedy 201, that would raise tariffs on imported steel to protect U.S. producers from the low-cost imports. Some criticized the move as running counter to the Bush administration's professed support for free trade. However, when countries are not trading fairly, retaliation with protectionist measures to level the playing field is sometimes considered appropriate.

An additional argument for protection is national security, for example, in the case of oil. The United States would not want to be totally reliant on imported oil in case of war or other circumstances that do not allow the United States access to oil. Promoting some degree of self-sufficiency in certain kinds of products is desirable.

Hidden Costs of Protectionism

The decision to protect local jobs at the expense of local consumers has costs. Consumers are harmed. When protections are established against lower-priced imports, the entire country may experience other economic costs. Economists have

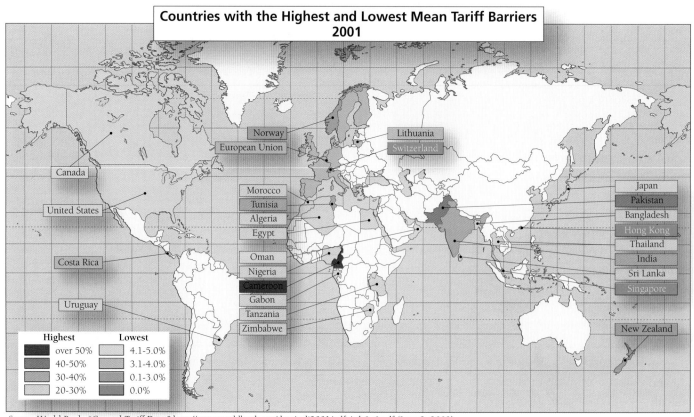

Countries with the Highest and Lowest Mean Tariff Barriers 2001

Highest		Lowest	
■	over 50%		4.1-5.0%
■	40-50%		3.1-4.0%
■	30-40%		0.1-3.0%
	20-30%		0.0%

Source: World Bank, "General Tariff Data," http://www.worldbank.org/data/wdi2001/pdfs/tab6_6.pdf (June 2, 2003).

calculated the cost of each job saved from a number of different protectionist measures. For example, they found that restrictions on imported motorcycles cost Americans $150,000 per year per job saved. The annual cost for saving a job in the auto industry was $105,000 per job. Clearly saving these jobs was very expensive. In these two cases, the actual salaries of the jobs saved are significantly less than the cost of retaining that worker. So why do we protect these workers at such a high cost?

The answer lies in the politics of protectionism. Politicians, not economists, determine trade policies. Helping these workers and these industries to fight foreign competition through tariffs or quotas permits tremendous gains while each individual consumer pays a very small cost. Although the total costs to all U.S. consumers can be quite large, the individual share is very low. Consumers usually do not complain when faced with higher prices; however, the industry and

workers affected by the lower-cost imports lobby very hard for protection.

Economists argue that the benefits of protectionism are less than the losses and that countries should not engage in protectionist policies. Politicians, however, often listen to the loudest voices, which usually come from those harmed from the imports. Workers also vote. Therefore, politicians protect these workers and businesses, often at the expense of the consumers and the country as a whole.

Further Reading

Aggarwal, Vinod K. *The Future of the Liberal Trading Order.* Berkeley, Calif.: University of California Press, 1992.

Carbaugh, Robert J. *International Economics.* 8th ed. Cincinnati, Ohio: South-Western, 2002.

Krugman, Paul. *The Accidental Theorist.* London: Penguin, 1999.

United States Tariff Data Base. http://dataweb.usitc.gov/scripts/tariff.asp (March 13, 2003).

—*Tracy Hofer*

U.S. steelworkers march near the White House in February 2002 in support of the steel industry's demands for a high tariff on imported steel.

Public Goods

A public good is a category of goods, also sometimes called collective goods, that are neither rival nor excludable. A good is rival if one person's consumption or use of it reduces another person's ability to enjoy it: if someone eats a slice of pizza, another person cannot eat the same slice. A good is excludable if people can be prevented from receiving the benefits of the good—particularly people who do not pay to receive the benefits. For example, to see a first-run movie, one has to buy a ticket; those who do not buy tickets are excluded. Rival and excludable goods are called private goods.

Most goods people consume are rival. If someone wears a coat, another person cannot receive the protection it provides. If somebody is riding in the front seat of a roller coaster, another person cannot experience the thrill of sitting there at the same time. If somebody harvests a whale out of the ocean, another person cannot harvest the same whale. However, many goods have benefits that can be shared or jointly consumed—these are public goods. The radio signal coming from a local rock station can be enjoyed by anyone in the area who has a receiver. The light coming from a lighthouse can be used by any ship along the coast to guide its passage. If swamps near a town are sprayed for mosquito control, everyone in the town shares in the benefits. Similarly, people can share the benefits of a large fireworks display, a television signal from an orbiting satellite, or a highway that has been cleared of snow.

Most goods people consume are also excludable. People who do not pay for the good are often easily excluded from receiving the benefits of the good. To enjoy a soft drink, one must put money into the vending machine. To wear a new designer shirt, one must pay the store cashier. To use a toll road, one must deposit coins in the toll basket. However, excluding nonpayers from receiving the benefits of many goods can be either too costly or simply not possible.

How could people who did not pay be kept from viewing a large fireworks display? Once a lighthouse is on for one ship, all ships are going to see the beacon. Similarly, once mosquito control has been provided, no way is available to exclude someone from receiving the benefits. Because a satellite signal can be scrambled, excluding people from receiving the benefits of the signal is possible, so this good is excludable and therefore is not a public good.

The Problem with Public Goods

If a good has the characteristics of a public good, then markets will likely produce too little of it. In fact, markets may not produce it at all. Because nonpaying users cannot be excluded from enjoying a public good, potential suppliers would have great difficulty collecting any payment for the benefits provided. This is the "free-rider" problem (see box). The larger the incentive for people to be free-riders, the less likely suppliers would be to collect enough payments to cover the costs of providing the good or service.

The Free-rider Problem

The people of Grand Falls, Minnesota, enjoy everything about their summers on the lake except the constant nuisance of mosquito bites. Pat, an entrepreneur, sees a potential opportunity. Pat knows of a spraying process that, if applied correctly, could reduce the mosquito population and problem. The cost of the application would be around $2,000. Pat further estimates that each person in this town of 1,000 would probably be willing and able to pay at least $5 to have this done. Suppose that this is true. Then the benefit of the application is at least $5,000 while the cost is only $2,000. As the benefits exceed the costs, the application would be a worthwhile (efficient) use of resources.

However, would it actually get done? Suppose Pat decided to charge each person $3 to provide this service. Is this a good deal for everyone? Clearly, the answer is yes. Pat would make a profit of $1,000 (the $3,000 he would collect minus the $2,000 cost of the application) and each person in the town would pay $3 for something that is worth at least $5 to them. Many people, however, will realize that they would benefit from the spraying whether they pay or not. The application is not an excludable good.

While getting the $5 benefit of the spraying for $3 is a good deal, getting the same benefit for nothing would be even better. People have the incentive to become free-riders. A free-rider is a person who receives the benefit of a good without paying for it. They hope others will pay for the good while they get it for free. Because everyone has this incentive, some and perhaps many of the residents would decide not to pay. Pat would probably not be able to collect enough money to cover the cost of the application and, accordingly, would not provide it.

If markets cannot be relied upon to provide public goods, the simplest remedy is for the government either to produce these goods itself or to pay to have them privately produced. The government is able to avoid the free-rider problem because it can force people to pay through its ability to tax. These tax collections can be used to cover the cost of providing the public goods. A look at the budgets of governments at various levels reveals expenditures on many different public goods.

At the federal level, national defense is perhaps the most obvious example. Wilderness areas and national parks are also public goods to the extent that they provide benefits (carbon dioxide absorption by the trees and habitat or species preservation) even to people who do not visit them. The federal government also subsidizes basic research through agencies like the National Science Foundation, the National

Institutes of Health, and the National Aeronautics and Space Administration because knowledge has the characteristics of a public good. At the state level, highways, education, and public safety—all of which have some public aspects—are provided. At the local level, education, snow

The beacon from a lighthouse is a public good because it benefits every ship that passes.

Some Types of Public Goods

- National defense
- National parks and wilderness areas
- Basic scientific research
- Space exploration
- Bridge and road construction
- Education
- Public safety
- Infrastructure maintenance
- Public celebrations

Planes fly over Marco Island, Florida, spraying insecticide to kill mosquitoes. This is considered a non-excludable public good because everyone on Marco Island benefits, regardless of whether they helped pay for the spraying.

plowing, fireworks displays, and even mosquito control might be provided.

Providing the Right Amount of a Public Good

Assuring that the government provides public goods efficiently is difficult. For example, is the federal government providing too much or too little national defense? Is the air quality over a city too clean or not clean enough? According to economists the efficient amount to provide is that amount where the net benefits (total benefits minus total costs) received by society are the greatest. Governments often resort to cost-benefit analysis to determine the correct level. Such an analysis looks at both the benefits and the costs of providing a public good.

Without markets, determining these values is difficult. For example, if the price of a candy bar is $1 and you see 10 people buy one, you can conclude that each of them considers the candy bar to be valued at $1 or more. Observing these price reactions for a public good is impossible because of the pricing difficulties described earlier. One could simply ask people what a particular good is worth to them, but they would be likely to exaggerate (depending on whether they wanted the good or not) because what they say would have little bearing on what they might actually have to pay. Government leaders are left to approximate the costs and benefits or adjust the quantities of public goods in response to political pressure from their constituents.

Even were the government able to accurately measure the benefits and costs of providing a public good and able to provide it at that exact level where net benefits are maximized, many people would likely still say it is not the right amount. With a private good people are able to adjust the amount they consume according to their individual tastes and the price of the good. Some people choose to have two sweaters, while others choose to have 20. With a public good, on the other hand, everyone is given the same amount and they cannot adjust the price they pay for it (the amount of taxes paid). As no one is free to adjust either the quantity or the price to their particular tastes and preferences, most are likely to be unhappy with the amount of the good provided. Thus, the debate over the appropriate amount of national defense, environmental quality, education, and other public goods never really ends.

Further Reading

Baumol, William J., and Alan S. Blinder. *Microeconomics: Principles and Policy*. 8th ed. Fort Worth, Tex.: Dryden Press, 2000.

Mankiw, N. Gregory. *Principles of Economics*. 2nd ed. Fort Worth, Tex.: Harcourt College Publishers, 2001.

McConnell, Campbell R., and Stanley L. Brue. *Economics: Principles, Problems, and Policies*. 15th ed. New York: McGraw-Hill, 2002.

—*Curt L. Anderson*

Public Relations and Marketing, Business Practice

Public relations (PR) and marketing campaigns play an enormous role in U.S. society by shaping the public's perceptions of everything from products to politicians to colleges. Every year corporations, special interest groups, and a host of other entities spend billions of dollars to influence the public's perceptions through PR and marketing.

Public relations is an organized effort to communicate with the general public or a specific subgroup. That effort might involve advertising, interviews on local media outlets, or direct mailings sent to people's homes. In most cases, the effort is focused on delivering a clear message or image to the public. For example, most colleges want to send future students and their parents a clear message about the strength of their institutions. They do this through college catalogs, campus tours, and orientation programs. All of those efforts are PR.

Marketing involves identifying and assessing people's needs and finding a way to fill those needs with anything from a new product to a political candidate. For example, to successfully market a new kind of shampoo the first step would be to survey the market, find what group of consumers is not having its needs met, and create a product to fill that need. At that point, the PR professional would create an image for that product and use various forms of advertising to convey that image to the consumer.

Designing a Campaign

The entire marketing and PR process may sound complicated, but the choices made throughout a successful campaign can be broken into parts. First, those involved in a PR campaign must determine exactly what they are trying to convey to the public. Every time anyone within the company or operation makes contact with the public, that is an act of PR. Good PR executives find a specific image that sets the product or firm (the PR company's customer) apart from other companies that perform the same service. Examples include focusing on customer service, improving the ingredients in its products, or keeping up with technology.

Customers should take away from any interaction with a company or institution an overwhelming sense of the chosen image even though most work is done behind the scenes and is very subtle. If a college wants to convince prospective students that it is a serious institution, tour leaders might show students the library and various classrooms. However, if the college wants to amend its conservative image and focus on how entertaining a student's life can be, the tour leaders might take prospective students to football games. If a cellular phone company wants to show customers that it has the

See also:
Advertising, Business Practice; Advertising Industry; Demographics; Market Research; Public Relations Industry.

Public Relations Tools		
Printed word	**Spoken word**	**Image**
• House publications pamphlets, booklets, letters and bulletins	• Meetings	• Films
• Newsletters	• Speeches	• Television
• Inserts and enclosures	• Public appearances	• Internet
• Advertising		• Displays and exhibits
		• Staged events

Source: Scott M. Cutlip and Allen H. Center, *Effective Public Relations*, 6th ed., Englewood Cliffs, N.J., Prentice Hall, 1985.

most extensive network available, the focus of its commercials and advertisements should be that message. On the other hand, the company might showcase its call-in help center if it wants to highlight efficient customer service.

Everyone within a PR operation should be clear about what the public should hear. In the case of a political candidate, what strengths will be stressed during media contacts and personal interactions with voters should be clear. In some cases, those strengths may be the competitor's weaknesses. If an opponent has made some questionable personal decisions, the idea of personal character might be chosen as a strength to be emphasized by political foes. Conversely, a candidate may decide to run a positive campaign and not bring up an opponent's bad behavior, in which case the decision to avoid negative comments can itself be touted in PR materials.

A successful marketing or PR campaign for a product must also convey a specific message. Choosing the perfect message for a product is difficult because the message must appeal to a variety of people and set the product apart from others like it. For example, a hot dog company probably should not focus on the nutritional content of the product, but should likely stress quick and easy preparation methods and the good taste. A PR campaign for organically grown produce should stress the healthy nature of the product and the benefits of consuming it.

A good PR and marketing campaign will make consumers' decisions for them when choosing which brand of product to purchase. A PR and marketing campaign, which includes the design of the product's packaging, should be memorable. The hot dog package should grab people's attention as they scan a row of hot dogs in the supermarket. The package should make consumers remember the advertising they have seen about the product and should make them interested in purchasing those particular hot dogs. The consumer should head to the grocery store with the product in mind after seeing advertising about its wonderful taste, health benefits, or entertaining nature.

Speaking to the Target Market

Once the message is clear, a successful PR team will set about conveying it to the public, first by choosing the target audience. This may involve market research to determine the spending habits of people, or it might involve internal assessments about the goals of the PR and marketing campaign. Creating an image and attempting to appeal to people who will likely have no interest in your product wastes time and money. For example, political candidates in one state should not spend much time crafting a message and advertising to appeal to residents in other states who cannot vote for them. However, many corporations make such mistakes in their marketing campaigns.

Another marketing decision is how much to charge for a particular product. How much can the target audience afford to spend? Who are your competitors in the market? Few people will pay several dollars more to purchase similar products even if the brand image of a certain product is stronger than that of another.

After target audience and price are determined, the next step is determining how to publicize the message and image. In

Goals of Public Relations Campaigns	
Type of Client	**Goal**
Product	• Improve sales • Increase earnings
Company or Institution	• Create positive feelings about company • Create impression of financial success
Politician	• Create strong image of the person • Instill image of superiority over other candidates

Race car driver Jeff Gordon has a variety of sponsorship agreements with different firms; he contributes to their PR and marketing campaigns simply by wearing his uniform.

some instances, direct marketing (sending information directly to the consumer) is most beneficial. Politicians mail brochures about their platforms during most national campaigns. In other instances, advertising on billboards, newspapers, magazines, television, or even the side of a bus might best convey the information. Successful PR executives work with teams of advertisers to best craft their message for the chosen target market.

Another marketing tool is placing the image, logo, or slogan on products available to the general public or the target audience. Companies often place their name on souvenirs given out at sporting events or even help sponsor the event itself. Successful market research should provide clues as to the best method. For example, because more men attend sporting events, putting a sports-drink company name on bottles at a baseball game is almost certainly more efficient than putting the name of a makeup company on the bottles.

Working with the Media

A successful PR campaign must include positive interactions with the media. In modern society, television, radio, newspapers, magazines, and the Internet all provide valuable outlets for conveying a message to the public. To get the media's attention, often a press release must be written to explain the issue or event. The release should include all critical information as well as phone numbers to contact for additional information. For example, a press release about an upcoming event should include a brief description of the event, the time, the location, and the purpose of the gathering. Also helpful is a letter with background information about the issue at hand.

In order to suggest a story to members of the media, it is often necessary to complete a pitch letter that includes a brief description of your idea and a case for why you believe it is newsworthy. Public appearances often draw media attention as well. Many politicians and corporate executives make several speeches a year in an attempt to draw positive attention to themselves or their company.

In all cases, PR and marketing teams want to attract the media for so-called positive press, which highlights in some way the success of an operation. However, a PR team must also be prepared for negative publicity that can come from either an opponent or a bad outcome. Companies must be prepared to show their strength during a financial crisis or in the case of a serious accident. PR teams are well advised not to hide from the media when a negative event occurs. For example, an airline should have a team prepared should a plane crash, so the company can show that it is both compassionate and in control of the situation.

In the case of financial hardship, sending a message about the renewed strength of the company is important. In some cases, PR experts will have to craft a new image for the company, but usually sticking with the same ideas and showing consistency are best. For example, when stock prices plummet on Wall Street, corporations often make optimistic statements about the future to reassure stockholders. A good PR operation can seriously contribute to the financial success of a large operation.

A successful PR and marketing campaign should have a number of goals. For a product, the campaign should improve sales and increase earnings. For a company or large institution, the campaign should leave the general public with a positive feeling about the company's interest in its customers and, for shareholders,

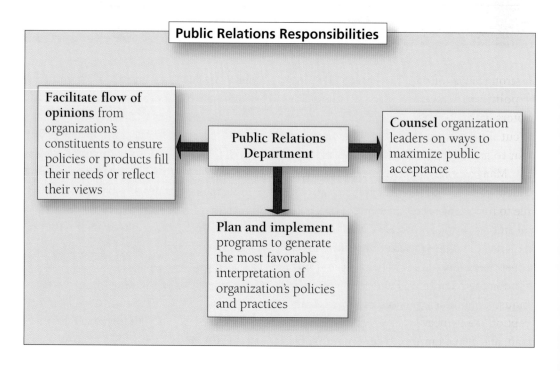

Public Relations Responsibilities

Facilitate flow of opinions from organization's constituents to ensure policies or products fill their needs or reflect their views

Public Relations Department

Counsel organization leaders on ways to maximize public acceptance

Plan and implement programs to generate the most favorable interpretation of organization's policies and practices

a strong sense of its financial success. For a politician, the campaign should leave voters with a strong image of the person as a cut above most and certainly far superior to any of his or her competitors.

Many aspects of PR and marketing entail much work behind the scenes and are invisible to the average consumer or voter. Almost all major corporations have their own PR experts. Other companies hire PR firms or consultants. Even the government and local school districts have PR employees. The industry continues to shape the public's perception about nearly every product, politician, and agenda in U.S. society.

Further Reading

Culligan, Matthew, and Dolph Greene. *Getting Back to the Basics of Public Relations and Publicity.* New York: Crown Publishers, 1982.

Cutlip, Scott M., Allen H. Center, and Glen M. Broom. *Effective Public Relations.* Upper Saddle River, N.J.: Prentice Hall, 1999.

Knesel, Dave. *Free Publicity: A Step by Step Guide.* New York: Sterling Publishing, 1982.

Parkhurst, William. *How to Get Publicity.* New York: Harper Business, 2000.

Ries, Al, and Laura Ries. *The Fall of Advertising and the Rise of PR.* New York: HarperBusiness, 2002.

—*Karen Ayres*

Bill Clinton at a campaign rally in Georgia, 1992. Political campaigns are, to a degree, battles of public perception, so PR and marketing are a key part of every political campaign.

Public Relations Industry

Public relations (PR) is the craft of creating favorable public opinion of a person, product, concept, or organization. Using both creative and scientific techniques, public relations professionals work to present their clients in a positive light. Because people's perceptions influence decisions about what businesses to patronize and what brands to buy, effective PR is integral to a company's success.

Public relations, marketing, and advertising are complementary marketing functions that often overlap: a public relations campaign may include advertisements designed to reinforce a positive public image, for instance. Advertising, however, seeks to persuade a consumer directly; PR typically reaches the consumer through favorable media coverage. For example, PR strategists for a food company may convince a news team to broadcast a feature story on the health benefits of olive oil, giving the public a rational reason to take notice of and to buy olive oil; at the same time, advertising professionals will develop ads to create interest on a more instinctive level, perhaps through showing the oil drizzling appealingly over a lush salad.

History of the PR Industry

Public relations as a professional industry began in the early twentieth century. Although General Electric was the first company to create a publicity department in 1897, the roots of public relations as we recognize it today can be dated to the Progressive Era. Muckraking journalists in the early twentieth century depicted big business owners as greedy, corrupt individuals who threatened both the autonomy and the personal livelihood of the average American. Company owners, in response, employed strategic marketing tactics to sway public opinion of big business toward the positive.

In 1906 Ivy Lee, a former newspaperman, became publicity adviser to several coal mine operators who had angered the press with their refusal to release information about the condition of their miners. In 1914 Lee gained professional renown for his assistance to the Rockefellers in providing damage control following the Ludlow massacre, in which striking miners and their families were killed over disputed mine interests. Lee was also employed by the Pennsylvania Railroad to act as an intermediary between officials and the media, releasing carefully selected information when necessary.

Although Lee contributed to the establishment of the PR profession, Edward L. Bernays is the individual credited as being

Phases of the PR Process

Research and listening: Probing opinions and evaluating attitudes

Planning and decision making: Plotting course of campaign

Communications: Communicating campaign

Evaluation: Assessing effectiveness of campaign

the father of public relations. During World War I, Bernays, a nephew of Sigmund Freud, worked for the U.S. government as its propaganda authority and served on the Committee on Public Information. He went on to instruct political leaders on the use of the mass media as a PR tool and the manipulation of audience consent. Both Great Britain and the United States had hired publicists, and, in 1913, U.S. legislation required congressional authorization to allocate government funds for publicity experts.

The PR industry, eager to legitimate its status as a profession, created associations, including the Public Relations Society of America and the Public Relations Consultants Association in London. Colleges and universities began to offer courses and even academic majors in the field. Boston University was the first to establish a School of Public Relations in 1947. By mid-century PR was firmly entrenched as an American

Edward L. Bernays, a nephew of Sigmund Freud and a founder of the PR industry, in 1981.

Careers in Public Relations

The public relations field has continued to expand as more and more individuals and businesses realize they must fight for the public's attention to ensure financial or political success. Public relations firms can handle a variety of clients or specialize in particular areas, politics or finance, for example. Large companies often have their own public relations staff that specializes in crafting the company's image and maintaining positive media relations.

Most people in public relations have a college degree either in communications or a related field like journalism. People with law degrees often do public relations for law firms and those with business degrees handle corporate public relations. Many public relations executives are former reporters who capitalize on their ability to answer reporters' questions. Many are writers with a knack for handling speeches and pitch letters.

—*Karen Ayres*

professional institution. Practices such as Hill and Knowlton and Whitaker & Baxter had become prominent companies alongside those of Lee and Bernays. With technological progress came new and innovative marketing techniques on which PR companies capitalized. Visual media, including short advertising films and commercials, became, and remain, the preferred method of marketing a new product. As the American demographic continues to change and vary over time, companies turn to the expertise of public relations firms to most efficiently address and cater to their consumer markets.

Activities of PR Firms

PR strategists pitch, or promote, ideas for various media including radio, television, magazines, newspapers, newsletters, and the Internet. The desired format varies by company and project: a bank may want to arrange a personal appearance, for instance, scheduling a loan officer to discuss interest rates on a talk show; a jewelry boutique may want a product placement, for example, convincing a movie star to wear a newly designed diamond bracelet to the Academy Awards. Feature articles, news stories, and online publications are prime formats for potential public relations exposure.

Media-savvy companies plan their initial PR campaign well before the doors first open for business. For example, a new store may combine a grand opening media event like a ribbon-cutting ceremony with advance interviews for industry publications to help frame public opinion. After the first campaign concludes, the company's marketing department (or its designated agency) will analyze results and use the data to help develop the next PR strategy. This process of planning, execution, and analysis will continue throughout the life of a company.

Public relations specialists strive to come up with ideas that the media can cover as legitimate news. The item may be newsworthy in itself, a new alternative fuel, for example, or it may be a manufactured event—the Miss America pageant, for example, was originally conceived as a way to extend the summer season in Atlantic City, New Jersey.

Whereas many PR strategies target either the media or the public, special events are usually designed to attract both. Trade shows, where companies in a specific industry gather to promote that industry and display their wares, call for public relations efforts targeted to the general press,

In 1922 Mayor Edward L. Bader hands the key to the city to the first crowned Miss America, Margaret Gorman, in Atlantic City, New Jersey. The original purpose of the pageant was to extend the tourist season in the resort town.

the industry press, and both current and prospective clients. Grand opening events and banquets are other examples of functions where company representatives build one-on-one relationships with both media and customers.

Companies may delegate day-to-day press releases to an in-house staff that also handles employee-relations activities like company newsletters. However, for special events and long-term publicity campaigns requiring coordination of several elements, businesses often retain a public relations firm. These PR shops may be stand-alone organizations, hybrid advertising and public relations companies, or parts of an advertising and marketing network. They offer clients specialized expertise, up-to-date lists of media contacts, the power of carefully nurtured media relationships, and a holistic approach that covers everything from market research to printing the company's logo on giveaway items.

In contrast, small businesses with limited budgets typically handle all public relations duties in-house. The total PR staff may be one person who squeezes the writing of an occasional press release into a schedule filled with other duties. Even so, small companies can accomplish impressive public relations feats through one idea person who displays the adventurous attitude and instinct for timing and flair for drama that attract the media. One California restaurant, for example, received extensive local coverage by passing out free hamburgers to workers repairing flood damage on its street and inviting the press to film the act.

PR activities encompass every area where the company touches the public. Because mass media play a large role in shaping public opinion, attracting media attention is a core function of PR. Media cooperation allows public relations strategists to craft an image that attracts the desired audience. However, this positive perception will be short-lived if it is not consistent with customers' actual experiences with the company.

Typical Goals of a PR Campaign

✓ Establish credibility for a product, organization, or point of view
✓ Define or strengthen a market position by emphasizing a unique benefit
✓ Build the perception that the company is a leader in its market
✓ Promote a change in direction
✓ Launch a new product or service
✓ Overcome negative publicity following an accident or scandal
✓ Keep a company in the public eye to ensure "top of mind" awareness

---

As the American public becomes more educated about the hazards of certain products—cigarettes and alcohol are prime examples—companies have scrambled to find new methods of marketing these products. For example, in 1999 Anheuser-Busch launched a public-service campaign against driving under the influence of alcohol. In doing so, the beer company both marketed its product effectively while responsibly making its clients aware of potential safety risks. Because of increased awareness of product safety, the tobacco industry has found marketing its product without acknowledging the many health risks increasingly difficult. Medical research firms have employed their own public relations firms to educate the public about the risks of smoking and to counter the ubiquitous marketing of the tobacco industry.

Although successful PR requires many sophisticated elements including research, strategy, analysis, and communications, at heart it is a simple appeal to human nature. As one practitioner has said, "We don't persuade people. We simply offer people reasons to persuade themselves."

Further Reading

Cutlip, Scott M., Allen H. Center, and Glen M. Broom. *Effective Public Relations*. Upper Saddle River, N.J.: Prentice Hall, 1999.

Levine, Michael. *Guerrilla P.R.* New York: HarperBusiness, 1993.

Wilcox, Dennis L. *Public Relations Writing and Media Techniques*. 4th ed. New York: Longman, 2001.

—*Dawn Dicker and Nicole Cohen*

Public Sector Unionism

Public sector unionism, or government unionism, refers to government employees who belong either to a union or an employee association that collectively bargains for wages. Two prominent public unions in the United States are the American Federation of State, County, and Municipal Employees (AFSCME), which has more than 1.2 million members, and the American Federation of Teachers, with more than 1 million members.

The proportion of privately employed workers belonging to unions in the United States has been decreasing for decades; in 2001 the proportion of privately employed workers covered by a collective bargaining agreement stood at 9.7 percent, compared with 18.5 percent in 1983. However, the proportion of government workers belonging to unions has increased significantly since 1980. The public sector unionization rate stood at 41.8 percent in 2001.

The growing prevalence of public sector unions may appear at first to be at odds with the historical development of unions in the United States. For most of the twentieth century, unions were associated with heavy manufacturing industries, where jobs can be

---

Who are Public Sector Workers?

Examples:
- Public school teachers
- Health care workers
- Mail carriers
- Firefighters and police
- Social service workers
- Legal, justice system, and prison employees
- Employees of public works projects (such as road building and maintenance)
- Librarians
- Air traffic controllers

---

difficult, unpleasant, and dangerous. The shift in unionization from the manufacturing to the public sector, where most jobs call for educated workers and involve office work, is actually consistent with the fundamental precepts of unions. Because higher wages can cause employment to fall, unions can bring the most benefits for their workers at the lowest cost by organizing at firms where the elasticity of labor demand is low—that is, where firms' hiring decisions are largely insensitive to wage changes.

Labor Demand in the Public Sector

When a union negotiates higher wages for its members, the higher wages can come at a cost of lower employment. When firms must pay higher wages, they may try to substitute machinery (capital) for the services of labor and may reduce output. Thus, when wages increase, employment tends to fall. Unions, as a result, are most successful in industries where the elasticity of labor demand is low. For instance, the airline pilots' union has been successful in obtaining wage increases without significantly affecting employment because machinery cannot substitute for a pilot, and the cost of pilots is low in relation to the cost of the capital involved in running an airline.

The demand for labor in the public sector is similarly insensitive to wage increases. Wages do not seem to affect public-sector employment much, and wage increases rarely result in layoffs. This is because the public sector is fundamentally different from the corporate world; governments are not trying to maximize profits or minimize costs. This fact has numerous repercussions. Motivating public-sector workers to act in the best interests of their employer (the government) can be more difficult than motivating private employees to act in the best interests of their employer. Job security tends to be greater in the public sector, and competitive pressures tend to be lower.

In the private sector, workers may receive large rewards for doing their work well. Valued employees receive raises, promotions, stock options, and greater job security. At the other end, poor workers can

be fired with little trouble. Government managers generally do not have that flexibility with their employees: wages are typically determined by education and tenure, and raises are generally given across the board. Also, firing problem employees in government service is exceedingly difficult. Managers, who also cannot be fired for poor performance, do not have the authority to decide raises or discharge problem workers because of the risk that managers will simply ignore the best interests of the government and give raises to friends and cronies.

Given the constraints that governments face in managing employees, union advocates argue that the presence of a public sector union might benefit both the government and the workers. Workers would naturally want a union because any wage increases they receive because of a union's efforts are unlikely to result in the elimination of their job. Government managers (and taxpayers) might find a public union desirable because of the ability of unions to mediate disputes between workers and managers that might affect employee performance and satisfaction as well as guard against cronyism.

What Have Unions Done for Government Employees?

Perhaps the most common complaint of government employees is that they are

New York City commuters walk across the Brooklyn Bridge during a strike of public transit workers in 1966.

The traditional position of many unions has been that it is management's job to manage and the union's job to represent the workforce in responding to those management decisions.

That position can no longer stand in today's public service.

There are too many forces threatening to weaken and hobble public services—well-orchestrated forces that can and need to be challenged. We must not and cannot accept that the decimation of public services is inevitable. As public service unions we must stop the tide of privatization, the deliberate weakening of public services and the outright sellout of the public's right to access quality public services.

In too many cases, governments are deliberately choosing to undermine pubic services. They do this by pursuing a domestic and international economic and social policy that directs public funds from public services into the pockets of wealthy individuals and corporations. . . . They do this by putting in place global trade agreements that effectively treat public services, programs and government protection of the public good to be unfair trade barriers. They do this by putting the rights of transnational corporations ahead of the public's right to public services that give people access to such fundamental human rights as education, shelter, health care and to a safe and clean environment.

For those who deliver public services, those who believe in them and understand their value, to stand idly by while this wholesale decimation continues would be at best negligent, at worst completely irresponsible. We have a responsibility not only to protect public services but also to fight for improved quality of service.

—Public Services International,
"Improving the Effectiveness of the Public Sector—If Not Us, Who?"
http://www.world-psi.org/psi.nsf/publications (February 20, 2003)

underpaid compared with the private sector. A cursory glance seems to bear this out: wages do tend to lag in the public sector, especially at the state and local level, and this gap has not appreciably narrowed since 1990.

However, government employees typically receive more fringe benefits than private sector workers. The pensions of government workers are more generous, on average, than private sector pensions, although the growth in popularity of individual retirement accounts like the ubiquitous 401(k) plans has lagged in the public sector. Other fringe benefits, vacation days, insurance, sick leave, and so forth, are generally far better in the public sector.

Government employees also have significant job security. The government sector rarely lays off workers, even during recessions. Indeed, the federal government often deliberately increases employment during a recession. State and local governments cannot run budget deficits and therefore are not able to use increases in government employment

to stabilize the economy, but they rarely close a budget deficit by reducing employment.

Do the higher benefits make up for the lower wages for government workers? The data seem to suggest that they do, at least for most public sector employees. For instance, the proportion of workers who quit a job to seek employment elsewhere is much lower in the public sector than in the private sector, according to the Bureau of Labor Statistics. Economists believe that the dramatically lower quit rates indicate that government employees are content to take lower wages in return for higher benefits and job security.

Impact of Public Sector Unions

In the private sector, union workers are generally thought to be more productive than their nonunion counterparts. In large part this is attributed to the idea of efficiency wages: higher wages attract better workers, and the opportunity cost of a worker losing his or her job from slacking

Constitution of the American Federation of State, County, and Municipal Employees
(Excerpt)

Objectives

The objectives of this Federation are:

A. To promote the organization of workers in general and public employees in particular.

B. To promote the welfare of the membership and to provide a voice in the determination of the terms and conditions of employment. We are committed to the process of collective bargaining as the most desirable, democratic, and effective method to achieve this. Both as union members and as citizens, we shall also employ available legislative and political action.

C. To promote civil service legislation and career service in government.

D. To provide research and educational services and activities designed to assist members and affiliates.

E. To foster cooperation among affiliates.

F. To cooperate with other labor organizations in particular and other segments of our society in general towards the end that the material riches of American society be more justly distributed and the moral promise of American life be realized.

G. To work with our brothers and sisters in other lands towards the improvement of the conditions of life and work in all countries, towards the diminution of international tensions and a reduction in the use of armed force to resolve disputes, and towards genuine fraternity of all workers.

off is higher. In the public sector, unions do not clearly increase productivity. Public sector unions are very heterogeneous: some have fought hard for performance bonuses and have worked with government to institute fair and impartial methods for penalizing poor workers, while other unions have opposed all forms of premium pay and any attempt to discipline workers outside the realm of the union.

As in the private sector, public sector unions have been successful in increasing compensation of workers as well as in shifting the nature of compensation from wages to fringe benefits. Public sector unions have probably not achieved the wage premiums associated with private sector unions, but at the same time they have had a much smaller impact on employment. Both results are attributable to the nature of the public sector rather than to the ability of the union management. Public unions have also had a small effect on the job security of government employees, mainly because job security was not an issue with government workers in the last three or four decades of the twentieth century.

Whether public sector unionization will increase in the future is unclear. Increasingly, the nonmilitary employees in the government are relatively well educated and mobile and thus would be thought to be less open to union organizing. At the same time, history seems to suggest that government employment will likely increase much faster than the general population. When unions show themselves to be successful at providing a service, workers generally seek them out, and most government workers have clearly received benefits from unionization.

Further Reading

Foster, Anne C. "Public and Private Sector Defined Benefit Pensions: A Comparison." *Compensation and Working Conditions* (Summer 1997): 37–43.

Freeman, Richard, and James Medoff. *What Do Unions Do?* New York: Basic Books, 1984.

Lichtenstein, Nelson. *State of the Union: A Century of American Labor.* Princeton, N.J.: Princeton University Press, 2002.

Lovejoy, Lora Mills. "The Comparative Value of Pensions in the Private and Public Sector." *Monthly Labor Review* 111 (December 1988): 18–26.

—J. Isaac Brannon

Publishing Industry

The U.S. publishing industry has three major categories: newspapers, magazines, and books, with a total of more than $100 billion in annual sales. In the last decade of the twentieth century, falling subscription rates have challenged newspaper and magazine publishers, and mergers have rocked book publishing. However, the growth of special-interest (niche) magazines, expansion in business and technical publishing, and promising electronic technologies suggest that the industry will retain its strong overall position in the U.S. economy.

The publishing industry dates to the mid-fifteenth century, when Johannes Gutenberg invented a printing press that used movable type. Publishing has been part of the American market since the first printing press was brought to America in 1638. Many of the founders of the United States were involved with the printing industry, most notably Benjamin Franklin, who published a wide variety of items—from newspapers and sermons to the first novel published in America.

The modern publishing era began with industrialization in the nineteenth century. Improved papermaking, typesetting, and printing technology greatly reduced the cost of producing publications, and the rapid spread of railways and telegraph lines made gathering information and distributing publications easier. In addition, increased literacy resulted in a large number of eager new readers.

Newspapers

The United States is one of the largest publishers of newspapers in the world, with approximately 1,800 daily and 9,700 weekly papers. The Newspaper Association of America

An undated colored engraving of Johannes Gutenberg in his workshop examining his first proof sheet.

reports more than 66 million daily and nearly 80 million weekend subscribers.

The modern newspaper age began in the 1830s, with the launch in urban areas of mass-market "penny papers" like the *New York Sun* and later the *Times*. By 1860 at least 3,000 weekly papers and more than 300 dailies were published; the *New York Herald* claimed a circulation of 77,000, making it the world's largest daily. The first U.S. news service, the Associated Press, was established in 1848. By mid-century major urban papers had regular news correspondents, and special correspondents provided vital coverage of the Civil War. Newspaper publishing empires also arose during this period, under Joseph Pulitzer (founder of the Pulitzer Prizes for journalism), Edward W. Scripps, and William Randolph Hearst. Pulitzer's *New York World* and Hearst's *New York Journal* engaged in a fierce rivalry, reaching 1.5 million readers each. Their sensationalistic coverage of the 1898 Spanish–American War began what became known as "yellow journalism."

Newspapers had their heyday in the early twentieth century. The number of papers peaked between 1909 and 1914, with about 2,600 dailies and 15,000 weeklies. Two additional news services, Scripps's United Press Association and Hearst's International News Service, were founded; they merged in 1958 to become United Press International. The early twentieth century also saw the launch of the first modern tabloid, the *New York Daily News*. Featuring dramatic text and numerous illustrations, by 1924 it boasted the largest circulation in the United States and paved the way for contemporary tabloids like the *National Enquirer*.

Circulation dropped off slowly after the 1920s. Despite the persistence of foreign-language papers and the emergence of specialty papers like the *Chicago Daily Defender* and *Pittsburgh News Courier* directed to African Americans, the newspaper industry began a serious decline in the 1960s. More people turned to television news, and the 1970s saw an unprecedented number of

	Number of establishments	Receipts (in million dollars)	Annual payroll (in million dollars)
Newspaper publishers	8,758	41,601	11,789
Periodical publishers	6,298	29,885	5,993
Book publishers	2,684	22,648	3,643
Total, publishing industries	33,896	179,035	43,358

Publishing Industry: Establishments, Receipts, and Payroll 1997

Note: Total includes other publishing industries not listed separately.
Source: U.S. Bureau of the Census, *1997 Economic Census*, October 1999.

newspaper closings and consolidations. By the early 1980s most major markets had only one newspaper left, and more than half of the remaining papers were owned by newspaper chains, including Gannett, Knight-Ridder, Advance Group (Newhouse), Scripps Howard, Hearst, Time Warner, News Corporation (Murdoch), and the Tribune Company.

However, the U.S. newspaper industry has again stabilized. National newspapers have emerged. *USA Today,* launched in 1982, reaches approximately 2.2 million readers, the highest daily circulation for a U.S. newspaper. Other national newspapers include the *New York Times*, the U.S. newspaper of record, with approximately 1.2 million readers; the *Wall Street Journal,* with approximately 1.8 million readers; and the *Christian Science Monitor*. Other newspapers with national presence include the *Boston Globe, Chicago Tribune, St. Louis Post-Dispatch, Miami Herald, Philadelphia Inquirer, Los Angeles Times*, and *Washington Post*. The emergence in the 1990s of a national advertising buying service has helped to increase advertising revenues, and a growing population of people over 35 is helping to steady circulation figures.

The popularity of the Internet as a vehicle for news delivery has brought new challenges and opportunities to the field. The first electronic newspaper, Ohio's *Columbus Dispatch*, went online in 1980; by 2000 nearly all U.S. newspapers offered online editions, and new Internet-only venues, for example, *Slate* and *Salon*, are available.

Magazines

Magazine publishing has a variety of different subcategories, including consumer magazines, which serve broad readerships through subscriptions and newsstand sales, and trade magazines, which serve specialized business, industrial, and professional readers. Association magazines, a third category, are sponsored by organizations and provided (usually free) to their members. According to the Magazine Publishers of America, more

The cover of Vanity Fair, *June 1914.*

than 17,000 consumer magazines were published in the United States in 2000, with the top 100 magazines in all categories reaching nearly 250 million subscribers. Circulation revenues for magazines in 2000 totaled nearly $1 billion. The major consumer magazine publishers in the United States today include Advance Group, Gruner+Jahr (Bertelsmann), Hachette Filipacchi, Hearst, Meredith, and Time Warner.

By the 1830s and 1840s pioneering American versions of many kinds of consumer magazines were available: the first woman's magazine, *Godey's Lady's Book*; the first intellectual magazine, *The Dial*; and the first illustrated magazine, *Leslie's Weekly*. Large circulation, general interest magazines appeared later in the century, notably *Harper's Weekly, Atlantic Monthly, Ladies' Home Journal*, and *The Saturday Evening Post*. At the end of the century, activist "muckraking" writers attacked social ills in *McClure's Magazine, Collier's,* and *Everybody's*.

The first half of the twentieth century was the golden age of general interest magazines. *Vanity Fair* and the *New Yorker* appeared in 1914 and 1925, respectively. Henry R. Luce published the first newsweekly, *Time*, in 1923; his magazine empire expanded to include such popular titles as *Life, Sports Illustrated,* and *Fortune. Time's* success spurred the launch of a competitor, *Newsweek*, in 1933.

As with newspapers, television eroded the market for general interest magazines; from the 1960s on, magazine publishers have concentrated on niche publications. In the 1960s John H. Johnson launched *Ebony* and a number of other magazines for African Americans; in the 1970s Helen Gurley Brown and Gloria Steinem moved women's magazines in new directions with the glamorous *Cosmopolitan* and the political *Ms.* Since 1990 the highest growth in the magazine industry has been in the areas of comic books and in magazines devoted to regional interests, lifestyle, management, the environment, computers and technology, and travel. However, the highest circulations have been achieved

Careers in the Publishing Industry

Writing and editing are the first occupations most people think of when considering the publishing industry, and they play a vital role in a book or article's production. The publishing industry currently employs nearly 388,000 writers, editors, news analysts, reporters, and correspondents. Although the main qualifications for a writing career may be talent or expertise in a subject, certain kinds of writing, particularly journalism, generally require an undergraduate degree in that field. Competition for jobs at large newspapers and publishing houses is always fierce, but opportunities abound with smaller newspapers, trade (business- and profession-related) publications, and online publications. Also, the need is growing for technical (scientific or technological) writers.

An editor's most important responsibility is helping to select the material his or her company will publish and evaluating the submissions of authors. Becoming an editor requires a college degree, if not in English or journalism then in a related field like communications or marketing. Editors must have an excellent grasp of grammar, usage, and style, as well as an ability to work under tight deadlines—this is especially true of newspaper or magazine editing. Strong writing skills and an ability to work under pressure are essential for all jobs in the industry. The ability to work independently is also important: unlike many industries, publishing has always relied on a large number of contract workers (freelancers and stringers) to supplement salaried staff.

Although writers and editors make up the backbone of publishing, the industry encompasses an array of occupations involved in every step of a book or other publication's production. Literary agents work with their author clients to sell their work to publishers and help to negotiate the best fees. Illustrators, graphic designers, Web designers, layout artists, and production managers are responsible for the arrangement of the content on the page and help shape the look and feel of every publication. Publicists, marketers, advertising agents, and salespeople help bring the books and magazines to stores and attract the notice of the public. Fact checkers, copy editors, and proofreaders work to screen the final text to make sure no factual or grammatical errors are printed.

by association magazines: the leader in 2000, with nearly 21 million copies, was the AARP's *Modern Maturity*.

Books
In 2002 the United States had about 3,000 book publishers. According to the American Booksellers Association, book sales in 2000 reached $25.2 billion. Book publishing includes consumer books (books sold in stores), educational, and professional books. Online retailers like Amazon.com have helped sustain consumer book sales, and an expanding college-age population has spurred sales in the educational market.

Concentrated in New York City, book publishing became an important U.S. industry in the early nineteenth century. Many of the most distinguished U.S.

imprints were born in the nineteenth century, including Harper; Merriam; Little, Brown; and Houghton Mifflin. Important twentieth-century imprints include Simon & Schuster; McGraw-Hill; Random House; Farrar, Straus, & Giroux; and Pantheon.

Probably the most significant development in U.S. book publishing was the emergence of mass market paperbacks in the 1930s, which made books more affordable. Pocket Books, Inc., the first American paperback imprint, was launched by Robert de Graff in 1939 and sold over 1.5 million paperback books that year. Over the next decade Bantam Books, New American

Production departments use desktop publishing to transform plain text into compelling layouts.

Library, and Fawcett World Library joined the field, followed in 1952 by Anchor Books. Paperbacks were originally used almost exclusively for reprints or for lower-prestige genres like science fiction. Only in the last few decades of the twentieth century did quality trade paperbacks appear; many new works of fiction and nonfiction are now published as quality paperbacks rather than as traditional hardcovers.

Book clubs have also expanded the industry. In the 1930s the Book-of-the-Month Club and Literary Guild helped bring books to readers who lacked access to bookstores or wanted help deciding what to read. Other mail-order book services followed, including *Reader's Digest*. Clubs have increasingly targeted special interests—romance, mystery, spirituality, and computers among them. In the 1990s talk-show host Oprah Winfrey took the book club concept to television, generating huge sales for the titles she selected.

Electronic publishing emerged in the 1980s and 1990s. Desktop publishing techniques and print-on-demand (POD) technology promised to reduce costs and accelerate production schedules. Many publishers launched e-book imprints. The banner year for e-publishing was 2000: the leading trade magazine, *Publishers Weekly,* added an e-publishing section; author Stephen King published a novel online, racking up 400,000 downloads in the first 24 hours; and industry analyst R. R. Bowker reported that more than 40,000 e-books were in print in America, representing over $1 million in potential sales. However, the potential sales have not been realized, and most publishers have scaled back their e-book programs. POD imprints—Xlibris is one—look more promising. With minimal production costs, POD publishers may be able to keep titles in print indefinitely, providing a valuable service to both authors and readers.

Prior to the 1960s most book publishers were individually owned and relatively small. When increased prosperity and higher college enrollments spurred predictions that Americans would devote more

time to reading, the first wave of public offer-
ings and mergers in the book industry
began. After a slowdown in the 1970s,
acquisitions accelerated again in the 1980s,
with foreign publishers becoming major
players. By the end of the 1980s, U.S. publishers were concentrated in the hands of
about a dozen corporations, and, by 1998,
most trade publishers were controlled by just
seven multinationals: Bertelsmann, Hearst,
Holtzbrinck, News Corporation, Pearson,
Viacom, and Time Warner. Simultaneously,
superstores like Borders and Barnes & Noble
emerged, and independent booksellers had
difficulty competing with the superstores'
selection and discounting.

Some critics have charged that a more corporate concern with profits has overwhelmed
book publishing's traditional dedication to
quality and diversity in publications, but others have noted the greater number of titles
available overall. New, smaller presses have
emerged to fill gaps left by the corporate publishers. Online sales, through Amazon.com
and others, have been robust, accounting
for 6 percent of all books purchased by

U.S. households in 2000. Furthermore, the
American Booksellers Association notes that
independent bookstores held their market
share between 1999 and 2000. The period of
upheaval may be ending.

Further Reading

Abrahamson, David. *Magazine-Made America : The
    Cultural Transformation of the Postwar
    Periodical*. Cresskill, N.J.: Hampton Press,
    1996.
Cohen, Daniel. *Yellow Journalism: Scandal,
    Sensationalism and Gossip in the Media*.
    Breckenridge, Colo.: Twenty First Century
    Books, 2000.
Graham, Gordon, and Richard Abel, eds. *The Book
    in the United States Today*. New Brunswick,
    N.J.: Transaction, 1997.
Greco, Albert N. *The Book Publishing Industry*.
    Boston: Allyn and Bacon, 1997.
Johnson, Sammye, and Patricia Prijatel. *The
    Magazine from Cover to Cover: Inside a Dynamic
    Industry*. New York: McGraw-Hill – NTC,
    2000.
Kilgour, Frederick G. *The Evolution of the Book*. New
    York: Oxford University Press, 1998.
Stephens, Mitchell. *A History of News*. Fort Worth,
    Tex.: Harcourt Brace, 1997.

—*Solveig C. Robinson*

*At a Barnes & Noble in
Bethesda, Maryland, shoppers
snap up multiple copies of
Harry Potter and the Goblet
of Fire in 2000.*

See also:
Hearst, William Randolph;
Publishing Industry.

Pulitzer, Joseph

1847–1911
Publisher

In the second half of the nineteenth century, Joseph Pulitzer was a renowned newspaper publisher and a powerful, influential journalist. Today he is remembered mainly for the prestigious prizes awarded in his name for achievements in arts and letters.

Pulitzer was born in Mako, now a part of Hungary, in 1847. His father, a grain merchant, was Jewish; his mother was a Roman Catholic. The Pulitzer family was wealthy, and Pulitzer attended private schools. When he was 17, he attempted to enlist in the Austrian army, the French Foreign Legion, and the British army, but he was rejected in each case because he suffered from bad eyesight and poor health generally. The resourceful Pulitzer succeeded in his attempt to join the military; he immigrated to the United States in 1864 to join the Union Army, serving as a substitute for a draftee during the Civil War. (U. S. law at the time permitted a draftee to avoid service by paying a fee or by providing a substitute to take his place.)

After leaving the service, Pulitzer moved to St. Louis, Missouri, where he worked as a baggage handler and a waiter while studying English. In 1868 Pulitzer took a job at the *Westliche Post*, a German-language newspaper, after he caught the attention of the paper's editors by critiquing a chess game they were playing in a library. Pulitzer quickly became known for his hard work as a reporter, and he was offered a controlling interest in the paper just four years later. Pulitzer became a publisher at age 25; by 1878 he had sealed a series of deals to become the owner of the *St. Louis Post-Dispatch*—a popular and respected publication to this day. Pulitzer also married Kate Davis, a socially prominent woman from Washington, D.C., in 1878.

Pulitzer suffered from poor eyesight, and in 1883 he planned a trip to Europe, where he hoped to gain relief by resting his eyes. During a stopover in New York he bought the *New York World*. The paper furthered Pulitzer's career in several ways. He used it as a forum for attacks on corruption that would become his journalistic signature. He pioneered the extensive use of illustrations in its pages. The *World* also introduced cartoons, sports news, and coverage of women's fashion, all new features designed to increase the entertainment value of the paper. His paper's sensationalistic approach to reporting—providing exaggerated accounts of wartime atrocities, for example—was designed to pique reader interest. The *New York World* also launched a campaign to raise money for the building of a pedestal for the Statue of Liberty in New York harbor. These various practices, both journalistic and promotional, were effective. The *World* became the country's largest newspaper, with a peak circulation of 600,000.

One of Pulitzer's competitors was Charles Dana, who published the *Sun*. Dana attacked Pulitzer personally, criticizing him

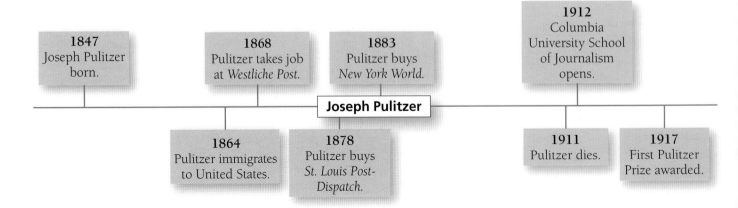

1847
Joseph Pulitzer
born.

1868
Pulitzer takes job
at *Westliche Post*.

1883
Pulitzer buys
New York World.

1912
Columbia
University School
of Journalism
opens.

Joseph Pulitzer

1864
Pulitzer immigrates
to United States.

1878
Pulitzer buys
*St. Louis Post-
Dispatch*.

1911
Pulitzer dies.

1917
First Pulitzer
Prize awarded.

as a Jew who had abandoned his people. These attacks were, in part, the reason for Pulitzer's leaving the *World* newsroom in 1890. He was 43 years old at the time and in ill health: nearly blind, severely depressed, and afflicted by a condition that caused him to be extremely sensitive to noise. He continued to control his newspaper, however—often working by means of coded messages he transmitted to his newsroom from soundproof rooms on his yacht.

Between 1896 and 1898 Pulitzer and the *World* staged an intense battle for readers against the *Journal*, which was operated by William Randolph Hearst. In their respective newspapers Pulitzer and Hearst sensationalized news so markedly that historians later credited (or blamed) them for having invented what became known as "yellow journalism." In truth, Pulitzer for the most part turned away from sensationalism at the end of the Spanish–American War and refocused his attention on government corruption. In 1909, for example, the *World* exposed a $40 million fraudulent payment from the United States to the French Panama Canal Company.

Pulitzer died on board his yacht in 1911. In his will, Pulitzer had specified that $2 million be given to Columbia University to establish a journalism school. Pulitzer strongly believed that journalists should be educated in schools specifically oriented to their craft. The Columbia University School of Journalism opened its doors in 1912, one year after Pulitzer's death.

Pulitzer's will also directed that part of his fortune be used to establish prizes or scholarships to encourage literature, journalism, and the advancement of education. An advisory board awarded the first Pulitzer Prize in 1917, and subsequent boards—typically including editors and academics as well as representatives from Columbia—have continued to serve in the selection process. Today, Pulitzer Prizes are awarded in 21 categories; about 2,000 individuals are nominated annually.

The number of awards categories has increased over the years. A cartoon prize

Our Republic and its press will rise or fall together. An able, disinterested, public-spirited press, with trained intelligence to know the right and courage to do it, can preserve that public virtue without which popular government is a sham and a mockery. A cynical, mercenary, demagogic press will produce in time a people as base as itself. The power to mould the future of the Republic will be in the hands of the journalists of future generations.

—Joseph Pulitzer, *The North American Review*, 1904

was added in 1922, along with an award for poetry. The first award for photography was given in 1942; the award for nonfiction was established in 1962. In journalism, award categories range from

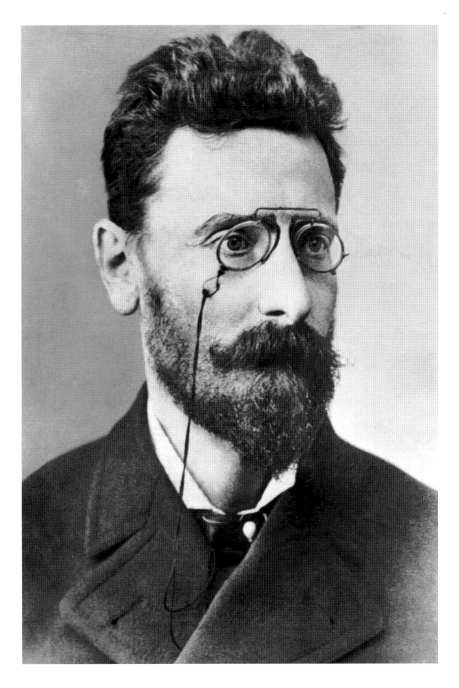

Undated portrait of Joseph Pulitzer.

JOURNALISM

1. For a distinguished example of meritorious public service by a newspaper through the use of its journalistic resources, which may include editorials, cartoons, and photographs, as well as reporting.
2. For a distinguished example of local reporting of breaking news.
3. For a distinguished example of investigative reporting by an individual or team, presented as a single article or series.
4. For a distinguished example of explanatory reporting that illuminates a significant and complex subject, demonstrating mastery of the subject, lucid writing and clear presentation.
5. For a distinguished example of beat reporting characterized by sustained and knowledgeable coverage of a particular subject or activity.
6. For a distinguished example of reporting on national affairs.
7. For a distinguished example of reporting on international affairs, including United Nations correspondence.
8. For a distinguished example of feature writing giving prime consideration to high literary quality and originality.
9. For distinguished commentary.
10. For distinguished criticism.
11. For distinguished editorial writing, the test of excellence being clearness of style, moral purpose, sound reasoning, and power to influence public opinion in what the writer conceives to be the right direction.
12. For a distinguished cartoon or portfolio of cartoons published during the year, characterized by originality, editorial effectiveness, quality of drawing, and pictorial effect.
13. For a distinguished example of breaking news photography in black and white or color, which may consist of a photograph or photographs, a sequence or an album.
14. For a distinguished example of feature photography in black and white or color, which may consist of a photograph or photographs, a sequence or an album.

LETTERS (BOOKS)

1. For distinguished fiction by an American author, preferably dealing with American life.
2. For a distinguished book upon the history of the United States.
3. For a distinguished biography or autobiography by an American author.
4. For a distinguished volume of original verse by an American author.
5. For a distinguished book of nonfiction by an American author that is not eligible for consideration in any other category.

POETRY

DRAMA

MUSIC

public service to criticism. The book category provides separately for awards in fiction, biography or autobiography, history, original verse, and nonfiction. Pulitzer Prizes are awarded every April by the president of Columbia University on the recommendation of the advisory board, after months of review.

Joseph Pulitzer was a hard worker, known for spending long nights on the job at his newspaper until ill health forced him to withdraw. He prided himself on having risen from a young man who could scarcely read English to his position of influence as a journalist and publisher. Pulitzer helped shape newspapers into their modern structure, and his name lives on in association with the highly coveted Pulitzer Prizes.

Further Reading

Brian, Denis. *Pulitzer: A Life*. New York: John Wiley & Sons, 2001.
Whitelaw, Nancy. *Joseph Pulitzer and the* New York World. Greensboro, N.C.: Morgan Reynolds, 2000.

—*Karen Ayres*

Randolph, A. Philip

1889–1979
Labor and civil rights leader

Ask most people, "Who led the 1963 civil rights March on Washington?" and the answer will probably be, "Martin Luther King, Jr." The real force behind the event, however, was the man who was not only the preeminent black labor leader of the twentieth century but also one of the fathers of the modern civil rights movement: Asa Philip Randolph.

An Activist Upbringing

Asa Philip Randolph was born April 15, 1889, in Crescent City, Florida, one of two sons of Rev. James William and Elizabeth Robinson Randolph, both descendants of slaves. His father was a minister in the African Methodist Episcopal (AME) church.

The Randolphs moved to Jacksonville in 1891, where Asa and his older brother, James, both graduated at the top of their classes at the Cookman Institute, the first high school for African Americans in Florida. In 1911 Randolph moved to New York City. Southern blacks and European immigrants were flocking to that city, and the new cultural and political ideologies of progressive reform, socialism, and communism found a

ready home. Randolph worked during the day and studied politics and economics at City College at night. Inspired by reformist orators like Eugene Debs, Randolph also joined the Socialist Party and became a stirring and popular soapbox orator.

In 1912 Randolph and his close friend Chandler Owen, a student at Columbia, founded an employment agency, and Randolph began organizing black workers. In 1917, following the entry of the United States into World War I, the two men founded a magazine, *The Messenger* (renamed *Black Worker* in 1929), that called for more positions in the war industry and the armed forces for blacks. In response to the race riots of 1919, Randolph and Owen formed the National Association for the Promotion of Labor Unionism among Negroes. After the war, Randolph lectured at New York's Rand School of Social Science and ran unsuccessfully for municipal and state offices on the Socialist Party ticket.

The Brotherhood of Porters versus the Pullman Company

In 1925 Randolph became founding president of the Brotherhood of Sleeping Car Porters (BSCP). The Pullman Company was among the most powerful business organizations in the United States, and it viciously resisted efforts to unionize its largely black staff. The BSCP needed help in organizing a union. Because Randolph

See also:
AFL-CIO; Civil Rights Legislation; Collective Bargaining; Labor Union; Public Sector Unionism.

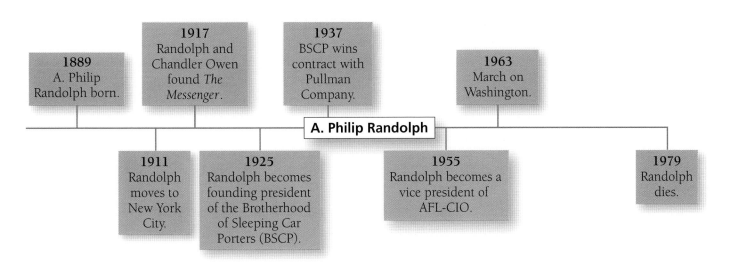

1889
A. Philip Randolph born.

1917
Randolph and Chandler Owen found *The Messenger*.

1937
BSCP wins contract with Pullman Company.

1963
March on Washington.

A. Philip Randolph

1911
Randolph moves to New York City.

1925
Randolph becomes founding president of the Brotherhood of Sleeping Car Porters (BSCP).

1955
Randolph becomes a vice president of AFL-CIO.

1979
Randolph dies.

was not a porter, he was immune from Pullman threats to his livelihood. For 12 years Randolph, the BSCP, and the Pullman Company fought over the right to organize.

Pullman used spies, threats, and firings, as well as a media campaign in the black press that branded the Brotherhood as communists. In the 1930s President Franklin Roosevelt's New Deal legislation guaranteed workers the right to organize and required corporations to negotiate with unions. Randolph requested formal affiliation with the American Federation of Labor (AFL) and was eventually granted an international charter.

In 1937 the BSCP finally obtained a labor contract with the Pullman Company. It was the first labor contract between a company and a black trade union. The following year Randolph removed the BSCP from the AFL in protest of its failure to fight discrimination in its ranks and took the union into the Congress of Industrial Organizations (CIO). With Randolph's urging, the CIO began to agitate on behalf of black labor unions.

Fighting for Equality in Defense Industries
Randolph next turned his attention to employment of blacks in the federal government

Outside the 1948 Democratic national convention in Philadelphia, protesters led by A. Philip Randolph (far left) demand equal rights and an anti–Jim Crow plank in the party platform.

1084 Randolph, A. Philip

and in industries with federal contracts. He was especially concerned about discrimination in the defense industry. With the nation preparing for war, many new jobs were available in defense, but blacks were barred from all but the lowest-paying positions.

Randolph began agitating for fair wages for blacks in the public sector. He warned Roosevelt that he would lead hundreds of thousands of blacks in a protest march on Washington, D.C. On June 25, 1941, Roosevelt issued an Executive Order barring discrimination in defense industries and federal bureaus and creating the Fair Employment Practices Committee.

When President Harry Truman called for a peacetime draft in 1947, but did not include a provision against segregation, Randolph founded the Committee against Jim Crow in Military Service and Training (changed to the League for Non-Violent Civil Disobedience Against Military Segregation) and called for blacks to refuse to register for the draft and refuse to serve if called.

After a tense year of demonstrations and meetings, Truman was eventually persuaded to issue an Executive Order banning segregation in the armed forces. Believing that blacks had achieved their purpose, Randolph called off the nonviolent civil disobedience campaign, thereby angering many young militants.

The Civil Rights Movement

By the early 1950s the civil rights movement was coalescing. The school segregation case, *Brown v. the Board of Education,* was before the Supreme Court in 1954 and the Montgomery bus boycott heated up in Alabama in 1955. Randolph continued to push for civil rights in government practices; nevertheless, blacks continued to have trouble in organized labor.

When the AFL merged with the CIO in 1955 (forming the AFL-CIO), Randolph was made a vice president and member of the executive council of the combined organization. However, the new organization began

A. Philip Randolph (front row, third from right) and other members of the Brotherhood of Sleeping Car Porters, circa 1930s.

*A. Philip Randolph
in New York City in 1966.*

rights movement. Bayard Rustin, one of the young militants who in the 1940s had denounced Randolph as a reactionary sell-out, made peace with Randolph and became the chief organizer. Trade unions previously opposed to civil rights were convinced to provide organizational and financial support, although Meany refused to endorse the march. Because of his popularity and lifelong commitment to labor issues, Randolph could serve as a bridge between the many different groups participating in the march and keep the coalition from splintering.

The March on Washington for Jobs and Freedom took place on August 28, 1963. It was an emotional event for Randolph, whose wife, Lucille, had died a few months before, and a turning point in the civil rights movement. After the march, Randolph, Martin Luther King, Jr., and other leaders met with President John Kennedy. Within a year, the Civil Rights Act of 1964 was signed. Two years later, Randolph formed the A. Philip Randolph Institute to provide funds for community leaders to study the causes of poverty.

After the march, Randolph's position as the elder statesman of the civil rights movement was secured. In 1968, suffering chronic illness, he resigned his presidency of the Brotherhood of Sleeping Car Porters and retired from public life. When he died in 1979, Randolph's funeral was attended by a host of political and civil rights luminaries led by President Jimmy Carter.

de-emphasizing its aggressive organizing of black workers. When Randolph stood to make his annual address against racism at the 1959 AFL-CIO convention, he was angrily rebuffed by AFL-CIO head George Meany. In response, Randolph and others formed the Negro American Labor Council (1960–1966) to fight discrimination within the AFL-CIO.

In 1963 Randolph again called for a march on Washington. This time the march would involve all the leaders of the civil

Further Reading

Anderson, Jervis. *A. Philip Randolph: A Biographical Portrait.* Berkeley: University of California Press, 1987.

Davis, Daniel S. *Mr. Black Labor: The Story of A. Philip Randolph, Father of the Civil Rights Movement.* New York: E. P. Dutton, 1972.

Harris, William H. *Keeping the Faith: A. Philip Randolph, Milton P. Webster, and the Brotherhood of Sleeping Car Porters, 1925–37.* Urbana: University of Illinois Press, 1991.

Reef, Catherine. *A. Philip Randolph: Union Leader and Civil Rights Crusader.* Berkeley Heights, N.J.: Enslow Publishers, 2001.

—Lisa Magloff

The labor movement has been the home of the working man, and traditionally, it has been the only haven for the dispossessed; and therefore, I have tried to build an alliance between the Negro and the American labor movement.

We must have faith that this society, divided by ethnicity and by class, and subject to profound social pressures, can one day become a nation of equals, and banish ethnic prejudice to the limbo of oblivion from which it shall never emerge.

Salvation for race, nation, or class must come from within. Freedom is never granted; it is won. Justice is never given; it is exacted. Freedom and justice must be struggled for by the oppressed of all lands and races, and the struggle must be continuous; for freedom is never a final fact, but a continuing evolving process to higher and higher levels of human social, economic, political, and religious relationships.

—A. Philip Randolph, 1969

Raw Materials

The dictionary definition of *raw material* is usually "material before being processed or manufactured into a final form." Although accurate, the definition barely touches the surface. Raw materials are the basis of all the manufactured, finished goods on which people rely in daily life. Literally billions of tons of raw materials are used annually to ensure a steady stream of automobiles, trucks, bathtubs, refrigerators, airplanes, milk cartons, doorknobs, surgical tools, paper clips, recycling bins, and myriad other objects, large and small.

Everything starts with raw materials. The basic building blocks for all raw materials are described in the periodic table of the elements. These elements compose all things—the ores and minerals we mine, the oil we pump, the crops we plant and harvest, and the trees we use for lumber or from which we extract, for example, maple sap to make syrup.

The supply chain for many raw materials begins with the mining of ores and minerals, including coal, iron ore, gold, silver, copper, and limestone. Other, lesser known ores also provide key materials for many manufacturing processes. These include bauxite (hydrous aluminum oxide needed to produce aluminum), manganese oxide, chromic oxide, and other metal oxides. Only a few elements appear in nature in a pure form—coal, gold, silver, and diamonds, which derive from coal, are examples. Most elements are molecularly tied with oxygen, silicates, or carbonates and are mined as such. Limestone, for example, is calcium carbonate; iron ore is iron oxide.

Crude oil is the raw material used to produce gasoline and diesel fuel; it is also the material basis for a huge petrochemical industry that produces thousands of products for industrial and consumer uses. These products include skin creams, household oils, and hair tonic.

Some raw materials are grown. A familiar example is corn. Not only is corn found on our dinner table and fed to livestock, it also serves as the main raw material for production of corn sugar, corn oil, furfural alcohol (a key ingredient in the manufacture of plastics), and other chemicals. Even the corncob

See also:
Agriculture Industry;
Commodities; Forest
Products Industry;
Manufacturing Industry;
Mining Industry.

Heaps of silica at a mine in western Australia.

comes into use as a raw material; it is ground and turned into a blasting abrasive material.

Basic heavy industry uses many raw materials. The steel industry, for example, is a major user of raw materials. High-tech equipment associated with the computer age also reaches consumers via raw materials and the manufacturing processes that convert these materials to new forms. One such raw material is silica. Seventy percent of the Earth's crust is some form of silica (silicon dioxide). The sand on most beaches is silica sand. Silicon metal does not occur naturally; it is produced from silicon dioxide. The process involves melting quartzite (silicon dioxide) rocks and coal at temperatures exceeding 3,000 degrees Fahrenheit. At such temperatures, the silicon releases its oxygen to the carbon in the coal, creating molten silicon metal that is poured into ingot molds. Upon cooling, the resultant product is pure silicon metal. Silicon metal is the basic raw material used in the manufacture of silicon chips for the computer industry; it is also used in silicone-based lubricants and is an important alloy used in the aluminum industry.

Silica sand is the basic raw material used by the glass industry. Glass is produced by heating silica sand to its fusion temperature (about 3,100 degrees Fahrenheit). In manufacturing windows, bottles, optical lenses, and other glass objects, the glass industry in the United States uses about 11 million tons of silica sand per year.

Not all raw materials are extracted from the Earth or grown in it. Some are extracted from previously manufactured goods. At the end of its useful life, for example, an old automobile can be crushed, yielding scrap iron that can then be reused in the production of

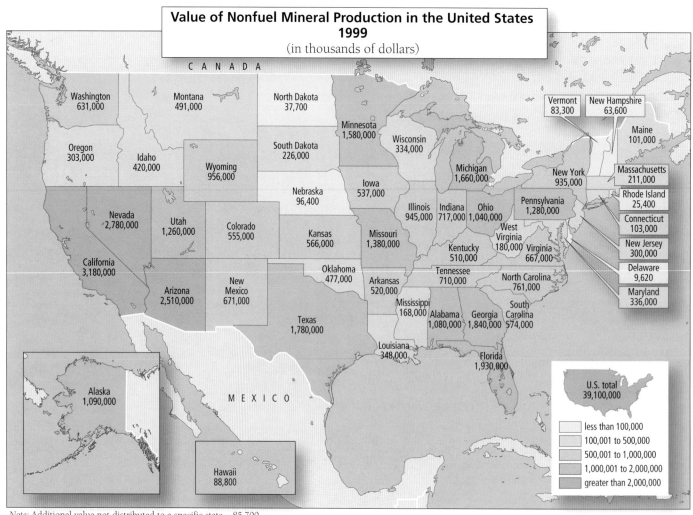

Value of Nonfuel Mineral Production in the United States 1999

(in thousands of dollars)

Washington 631,000
Montana 491,000
North Dakota 37,700
Vermont 83,300
New Hampshire 63,600
Maine 101,000
Oregon 303,000
Idaho 420,000
Wyoming 956,000
Minnesota 1,580,000
Wisconsin 334,000
South Dakota 226,000
Michigan 1,660,000
New York 935,000
Massachusetts 211,000
Nebraska 96,400
Iowa 537,000
Illinois 945,000
Indiana 717,000
Ohio 1,040,000
Pennsylvania 1,280,000
Rhode Island 25,400
Nevada 2,780,000
Utah 1,260,000
Colorado 555,000
Kansas 566,000
Missouri 1,380,000
West Virginia 180,000
Virginia 667,000
Connecticut 103,000
New Jersey 300,000
California 3,180,000
Kentucky 510,000
Delaware 9,620
Arizona 2,510,000
New Mexico 671,000
Oklahoma 477,000
Arkansas 520,000
Tennessee 710,000
North Carolina 761,000
Maryland 336,000
Texas 1,780,000
Mississippi 168,000
Alabama 1,080,000
Georgia 1,840,000
South Carolina 574,000
Louisiana 348,000
Florida 1,930,000
Alaska 1,090,000
Hawaii 88,800

MEXICO
CANADA

U.S. total 39,100,000

less than 100,000
100,001 to 500,000
500,001 to 1,000,000
1,000,001 to 2,000,000
greater than 2,000,000

Note: Additional value not distributed to a specific state = 85,700.
Source: U.S. Geological Survey, *Statistical Summary Annual Review,* 2000.

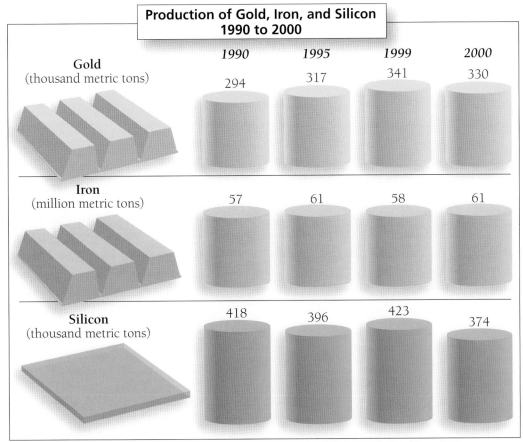

**Production of Gold, Iron, and Silicon
1990 to 2000**

	1990	1995	1999	2000
Gold (thousand metric tons)	294	317	341	330
Iron (million metric tons)	57	61	58	61
Silicon (thousand metric tons)	418	396	423	374

Source: U.S. Bureau of the Census, "Mineral Production: 1990 to 2000," *Statistical Abstracts of the United States,* 2001, http://www.census.gov/prod/2002pubs/01statab/natresor.pdf (April 3, 2003).

new steel. Scrap iron is used as a raw material in many industries. In fact, the basic metal industries like steel and metal casting are the largest recyclers in the world, taking metal that has been discarded and turning it into new, finished goods. In the United States, for example, 90 percent of a new cast-iron engine block is built from recycled iron.

Information about raw materials and their many uses is available at the Web site of the U.S. Geological Survey, a branch of the U.S. Department of the Interior. The site (www.usgs.gov) provides links to minerals publications and mineral commodity summaries. The U.S. Geological Survey keeps track of many minerals mined and used by industries in the United States—showing, for example, that more than 300,000 tons of gold are mined each year from 60 major lode mines in the United States (most of them in Alaska). The annual value of this mine production is about $3 billion. U.S. Geological Survey data also show that more than 60 million tons of iron ore are shipped every year from mines in Minnesota, Michigan, and six other states. Annual sales of this iron ore are estimated at $1.7 billion.

Many colleges and universities in the United States offer materials science courses and programs within their engineering programs. Materials science students study all aspects of materials used in manufacturing. They learn about mining, metallurgy, plastics, and other topics related to raw materials as they are used in industry and by consumers. Once mastered, this often overlooked field of study can lead to excellent jobs. Opportunities include work for design engineers, quality assurance personnel, laboratory technicians, and other technical positions in mining and manufacturing.

Further Reading

American Foundry Society. *Metal Casters Reference and Guide.* Des Plaines, Ill.: American Foundry Society, 1989.

Lide, D. R., ed. *Handbook of Chemistry and Physics.* Boca Raton, Fla.: CRC Press, 2001.

—Thomas H. Davies

Real Estate Industry

The real estate industry has two branches: residential and commercial. The residential real estate industry's agents and brokerages guide individuals through what is often the biggest financial transaction of their life—buying or selling a home. Commercial real estate involves the buying and selling of commercial properties, for example, office and apartment buildings and shopping centers. Although the basics of real estate transactions are the same for both kinds of real estate, the residential and commercial real estate industries differ greatly and are best considered separately.

Residential Real Estate

The concept and reality of a real estate agent dates to the mid-nineteenth century. Prior to that time, residential real estate transactions were completed by individuals well accustomed to handling money and property, usually lawyers, bankers, and businessmen (or, in rural areas, by two people using the barter system and a handshake). As real estate transactions grew larger and became more complex, real estate brokerages developed, offering the benefit of reliable market information and experience for a small commission.

By the early 1890s real estate agents and brokerages sought to create a national real estate group to unite the industry. After several failed attempts, what is now known as the National Association of Realtors was

A real estate agent shows properties to potential buyers. Large real estate firms often do more than show and sell houses; they also offer mortgages, insurance, and other services.

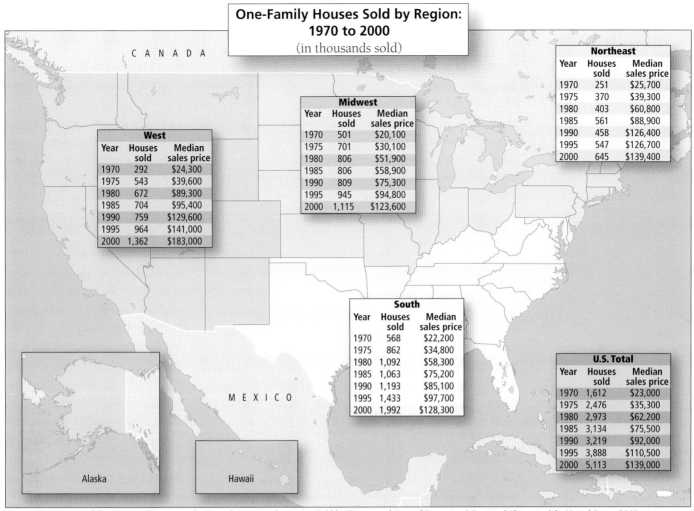

One-Family Houses Sold by Region: 1970 to 2000

(in thousands sold)

West

Year	Houses sold	Median sales price
1970	292	$24,300
1975	543	$39,600
1980	672	$89,300
1985	704	$95,400
1990	759	$129,600
1995	964	$141,000
2000	1,362	$183,000

Midwest

Year	Houses sold	Median sales price
1970	501	$20,100
1975	701	$30,100
1980	806	$51,900
1985	806	$58,900
1990	809	$75,300
1995	945	$94,800
2000	1,115	$123,600

Northeast

Year	Houses sold	Median sales price
1970	251	$25,700
1975	370	$39,300
1980	403	$60,800
1985	561	$88,900
1990	458	$126,400
1995	547	$126,700
2000	645	$139,400

South

Year	Houses sold	Median sales price
1970	568	$22,200
1975	862	$34,800
1980	1,092	$58,300
1985	1,063	$75,200
1990	1,193	$85,100
1995	1,433	$97,700
2000	1,992	$128,300

U.S. Total

Year	Houses sold	Median sales price
1970	1,612	$23,000
1975	2,476	$35,300
1980	2,973	$62,200
1985	3,134	$75,500
1990	3,219	$92,000
1995	3,888	$110,500
2000	5,113	$139,000

Source: U.S. Bureau of the Census, "New Privately-Owned One-Family Houses Sold by Region and Type of Financing," *Statistical Abstracts of the United States,* 2001.

founded in Chicago, Illinois, in 1908. The group addressed issues like uniform commission rates, standards of service, fair competition, and introduced the concept of shared listings.

In the early days real estate agents carried their property listings on index cards and gathered together on specific dates to exchange information. By the 1920s this exchange (multiple listing) was common practice. Over the next several decades local groups of realtors came together to create multiple listing services (MLS)—including printed catalogs—to facilitate the locating of sellers and the finding of buyers. The first computerized MLS database systems began operation in the mid-1970s.

The advent and widespread use of MLS computer databases and listing printouts coincided with the real estate boom of the late 1970s; the most well-known and dominant

real estate firms, for example, RE/MAX, ERA, and Century 21 (which is now the largest residential real estate firm, with more than 6,660 franchises worldwide), were also established in the late 1970s. Earlier, residential real estate was, for the most part, a local business handled by entrepreneurs. As the larger firms continued to grow in the 1980s, they came to dominate the real estate market.

Because of their size, the national real estate agencies were able to weather the boom–bust real estate cycles of the 1980s and early 1990s, which threatened many small and midsize local agencies across the nation. Still, as the market settled in various areas, many home buyers—especially first-time home buyers—turned to individual agents and small firms, most often drawn by the personal, one-on-one attention that the larger firms did not offer.

By the mid-1990s big firms like Century 21 began to focus on becoming one-stop shopping businesses. By offering in-house mortgage approval, insurance services, and legal advice (as well as having specialized relationships with inspectors and title agencies), the large firms were able to streamline real estate transactions, reducing time and cost and eliminating problems—a highly valuable service during the purchase or sale of a home.

The Internet forever changed real estate. In 2000 the National Association of Realtors' reported that nearly 40 percent of home buyers first learned about their new homes on the Internet, nearly equal to those who learned about their homes through newspaper ads. Prospective home buyers used Web sites—the National Association of Realtor's site (www.realty.com) is one—to learn the basics of real estate transactions and mortgages, locate realtors and lenders, and research properties according to specific details, for instance, price, zip code, amenities, and even school districts. The real estate Web sites cut down the legwork for real estate agents, who can arrive at a prospective

New houses under construction in O'Fallon, Missouri, in 2001.

home buyer's residence or office and teach him or her how to find—and even finance—a home online.

Other Web sites have scrapped the one-stop shopping model entirely. These firms, including www.helpusell.net, offer bare-bones services that are one step above a for-sale-by-owner real estate transaction. For a flat fee, the firms offer a for-sale sign, Web listing with photos, and an MLS listing, while the client prices the home and negotiates the transaction, most often using his or her own lawyer.

As the Internet and online MLS listings have helped make transactions more efficient, real estate brokerages that were built on their ability to offer market information find themselves with fewer customers. The real estate industry as a whole is also threatened by a proposal, drafted by the Federal Reserve and U.S. Treasury Department in 2001; this proposal would allow banks and other financial institutions to offer real estate brokerage and relocation services, introducing a new source of competition that is sure to change the nature of the real estate industry once again.

The Empire State Building, opened officially in 1931, remains one of the most prestigious pieces of commercial real estate in New York City.

Commercial Real Estate

The ownership of private property and the collection of rents from tenants are as old as civilization itself. The U.S. commercial real estate industry in its current form has been around only since the 1990s, however.

For most of U.S. history, office buildings, warehouses, shopping malls, apartment buildings, and other commercial properties were held in private hands. The industry was often described as "colorful," populated as it was by fast-talking, risk-taking developers like Donald Trump, who built buildings using mostly borrowed money and looked for tenants afterward, a practice known as speculative development.

The most successful developers were those with the best local connections to big commercial tenants, banks and other lenders, brokers, and other intermediaries. Great numbers of office buildings were amassed by individuals and private families who dominated single cities, including the Rudin, Mendik, Durst, and Speyer families of New York City, the Pritzkers and Rubloffs of Chicago, and the Cabots of Boston. Developers usually sold their properties to pension funds, insurance companies, and other large institutions looking for stable, long-term investments.

Commercial real estate is actually quite risky and subject to repeated boom-and-bust cycles. In a typical cycle, money poured forth from banks and insurance companies to fund speculative developments as the economy grew, often leading to a glut of supply as demand tapered off. One of the most extreme cycles in U.S. history occurred in the 1980s and was made worse by ill-advised government policies. The 1981 Economic Recovery Tax Act provided huge tax write-offs on even small real estate investments. The next year's Garn–St. Germain Act allowed savings and loan institutions to make loans on risky commercial real estate developments. Those twin incentives helped blast office-building completions in 1982 up 30 percent from the prior year. New construction piled on an added 580 million square feet of office space through 1987, with little regard to growth in demand.

When a 1986 tax reform law revoked the incentives and regulators finally and zealously clamped down on the savings and loans, the country had vacancy rates approaching 20 percent ready to greet the big employment slowdown that came three years later. The glut in the commercial real estate market was enormous, and many investors lost equally enormous amounts of money. Collapsing property prices bankrupted the savings and loan industry.

The 1990s brought changes. Commercial banks reduced construction lending and began to enforce much more stringent underwriting standards. In addition, a growing proportion of U.S. real estate is held in the hands of publicly traded companies, mostly real estate investment trusts (REITs).

Value of New Construction 1980 to 2000
(in millions of dollars)

Year	Residential buildings	Nonresidential buildings	Total
1980	175,822	129,275	364,101
1981	162,706	140,569	361,069
1982	134,605	145,054	333,894
1983	195,028	131,289	375,193
1984	231,396	155,261	437,325
1985	234,955	178,925	463,854
1986	266,481	163,740	479,623
1987	267,063	169,363	479,575
1988	263,385	164,191	467,599
1989	252,745	169,173	463,541
1990	228,943	167,896	436,999
1991	197,526	135,389	378,245
1992	232,134	120,921	401,567
1993	249,763	118,988	415,565
1994	274,966	127,576	445,414
1995	251,953	141,218	436,738
1996	281,207	155,813	476,650
1997	280,720	167,610	487,197
1998	287,960	177,644	519,859
1999	317,232	173,418	540,159
2000	323,708	179,654	555,089

Source: U.S. Bureau of the Census, "Value of New Construction," *Statistical Abstracts of the United States,* 2001.

REITs have existed since 1960 to allow small investors to invest in office buildings, shopping malls, and other commercial property. In their early decades, REITS were considered confusing and structurally flawed and were not an important factor in the real estate industry.

The 1986 tax law also reformed REITS, allowing them to operate much like other U.S. companies, with a chief executive officer, chief financial officer, and other full-time employees. The main distinguishing feature of REITs is that, unlike other corporations, they do not pay corporate income taxes. Instead, REITS are required to return more than 90 percent of their taxable income to investors in the form of quarterly dividends (cash payments distributed every three months).

Under this structure, REITs have become increasingly popular among individual and institutional investors attracted to their higher-than-normal dividend payments. REITs are now among the largest single owners of private property in the United States, replacing insurance companies and pension funds. The largest office building owner is the Chicago-based Equity Office Properties Trust, with more than 125 million square feet. Equity Residential Properties Trust, also based in Chicago, is among the largest apartment owners, with more than 1,000 buildings in 36 states. Both were founded by billionaire investor Sam Zell, who remains chairman of both firms. Simon Property Group, Inc., based in Indianapolis, Indiana, is the nation's largest mall owner and owns or has an interest in more than 252 shopping malls and strip developments.

The real estate industry is now more closely monitored. The industry's chronic boom-and-bust cycles had been blamed to a great degree on its secretive nature. Industry participants were largely in the dark about what their competitors were doing and had scant access to such key information as current and forecast vacancy rates, the amount of new supply under construction at a specific time in a given city, and the current

Careers in the Real Estate Industry

In the residential sphere, real estate agents tend either to work for national franchises like Century 21 or they may own their own small real estate business and operate locally. Commercial real estate has traditionally been dominated by private entrepreneurs who build and acquire multifamily homes, small office buildings, and retail strip centers using their own and borrowed capital. Other careers include:

LEASING BROKER
An intermediary usually hired by a property owner to market space to tenants. Major brokerage firms include CB Richard Ellis Services, Inc., based in Los Angeles, and Insignia/ESG, a unit of Insignia Financial Group, Inc., New York. In addition, large real estate companies often employ their own leasing specialists.

PROPERTY MANAGEMENT
Executives who specialize in operating large commercial properties, including maintenance, security, and other tenant services. Firms in this field include all large real estate companies, plus third-party property managers like Trammell Crow Co. of Dallas and Jones Lang LaSalle, Inc., Chicago.

PORTFOLIO MANAGER
Financial specialists who manage the real estate assets of pension funds and other institutional investors that directly own real estate. Large companies in this field are Lend Lease Real Estate Investment Management, Inc., a unit of Australia's Lend Lease Corp., AEW Capital Management LP, Boston, and RREEF, based in Chicago, acquired in 2002 by Deutsche Bank.

—Dean Starkman

demand for offices, apartments, warehouses, and retail space.

Public scrutiny has helped the whole industry. By the time the economic downturn that began in the spring of 2001 had taken hold, real estate developers had already begun to scale back plans for new construction. Vacancy rates rose, but far less than they had in other downturns and to less ill effect. The increased vacancies were attributed largely to job cuts and the general cutbacks in spending by U.S. corporate tenants.

Further Reading

Adler, Jerry. *High Rise: How 1,000 Men and Women Worked around the Clock for Five Years and Lost $200 Million Building a Skyscraper.* New York: Harper Collins, 1994.

The Journal of Real Estate Research. http://business.fullerton.edu/journal (March 17, 2003).

Pacelle, Mitchell. *Empire: A Tale of Obsession, Betrayal, and the Battle for an American Icon.* New York: John Wiley & Sons, 2001.

Shachtman, Tom. *Skyscraper Dreams: The Great Real Estate Dynasties of New York.* Boston: Little, Brown, 1991.

—Laura Lambert and Dean Starkman

Recession

A recession is a downturn in a nation's economy. More precisely, it is a decline in a nation's gross domestic product (GDP)—a nation's total expenditure on all goods and services produced in its economy—for six months or more. Nine recessions have occurred in the United States since 1950, including one that began in 2001.

An expanding economy, one in which the GDP is growing, creates jobs, rising wages, and steady prices. These conditions give a sense of stability, confidence in the future, and optimism, encouraging people to invest their resources and engage in productive activity. Society benefits as goods and services become cheaper while wages increase. Recessions reverse these positive conditions. In recessions, unemployment increases, wages fall, and overall confidence suffers.

The causes of upturns and downturns in the economy are not well understood. One theory postulates that they result from events that affect specific companies or industries initially but then, through a "ripple effect," have broader impact. For example, in the early twentieth century Henry Ford perfected techniques for the mass production of cars, which created jobs as new workers were needed to both produce and subsequently maintain those cars. Other industries, including steel, road construction, and oil production, expanded because of the new technology, creating yet more jobs. The new jobs increased the earning power of workers and their ability to buy new goods and services; they produced economic growth.

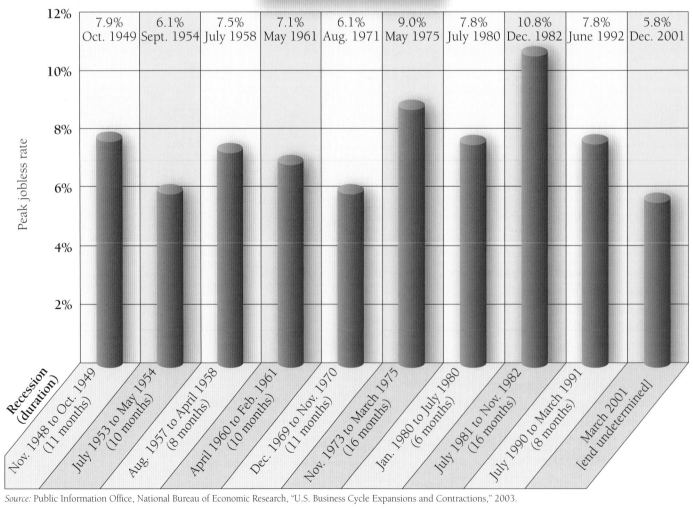

U.S. Recessions since 1950

Peak jobless rate

| 7.9% Oct. 1949 | 6.1% Sept. 1954 | 7.5% July 1958 | 7.1% May 1961 | 6.1% Aug. 1971 | 9.0% May 1975 | 7.8% July 1980 | 10.8% Dec. 1982 | 7.8% June 1992 | 5.8% Dec. 2001 |

Recession (duration)

Nov. 1948 to Oct. 1949 (11 months) | July 1953 to May 1954 (10 months) | Aug. 1957 to April 1958 (8 months) | April 1960 to Feb. 1961 (10 months) | Dec. 1969 to Nov. 1970 (11 months) | Nov. 1973 to March 1975 (16 months) | Jan. 1980 to July 1980 (6 months) | July 1981 to Nov. 1982 (16 months) | July 1990 to March 1991 (8 months) | March 2001 [end undetermined]

Source: Public Information Office, National Bureau of Economic Research, "U.S. Business Cycle Expansions and Contractions," 2003.

This process may also operate in reverse. If workers and company owners in a particular industry suffer a setback causing widespread losses of earnings and jobs, they will cut back on spending, and the ripple effect might push the economy toward or into a recession. One such recession occurred in 1973. Overseas oil producers colluded to increase prices dramatically. Demand for goods that used petroleum products dropped in response as the price for these goods rose. American car manufacturers were forced to reduce production of low-mileage vehicles that consumers no longer wanted. Hundreds of thousands of workers became unemployed in the automobile industry and in related industries; the entire economy went into a recession.

Another theory, developed by John Maynard Keynes, holds that recessions occur when people begin to spend less of their income. Events like the terrorist attacks in the United States on September 11, 2001, reduce optimism. Consumers lose confidence, saving more and spending less. Businesses react by reducing investment and employment. Unemployment then rises, wages fall, and the economy enters a recession. In these cases a recession might be said to occur because people acted as if one would occur.

The Great Depression of the 1930s is an excellent example. (A depression is a deep, prolonged economic downturn.) The decade of the 1920s was generally a period of optimism in the United States. People invested heavily and spent willingly on new consumer products. Businesses expanded, building new factories and hiring more workers, because consumers were willing to spend. The mood changed when the stock market crashed on October 29, 1929. Many investors suffered heavy losses and were unable to repay loans. Consequently, many banks were forced to close; many depositors lost their savings because their accounts were not insured. In the panic that followed, unemployment soared, spending dropped sharply, and the economy shrank dramatically. Government efforts to fix the

economy did not work, and employment rates and consumer confidence remained low until the United States entered World War II in 1941.

The U.S. government uses several methods to try to prevent recessions. First, it serves as a guarantor of economic stability. It protects the value of currency, acts as a lender of last resort to banks, and guarantees (through a program of federal insurance) the security of bank deposits. All of

The gas crisis of the 1970s pushed the U.S. economy deep into recession.

UNCHY, JUICY HOT DOGS AND FRUITY DRINKS

Recession Special!
SAVE 70¢
WE ARE POLITE NEW Y...

Gray's Papaya hot dog stand in November 2001 on New York's Upper West Side.

these measures foster economic confidence and optimism. Second, through the Federal Reserve system, the government monitors the economy and takes action to limit recessions when they do occur. It does this primarily through monetary policy. Monetary policy decisions made by the Federal Reserve Board of Governors have the effect of controlling the money supply. If a recession appears likely, the Fed has the power to purchase securities and to reduce the interest rates charged when banks borrow money at Federal Reserve district banks. These actions are intended to get more money into circulation, thus encouraging lending and giving businesses and consumers a greater incentive to spend and invest. The stimulus provided by increased spending and investment may then reignite economic growth.

Adjusting monetary policy does not always work. Six months or more may be needed for policy actions to take effect. To take timely, effective action, therefore, policy makers must try to predict future economic events. Often they are unable to provide accurate forecasts and, accordingly, fail to act in time to prevent a recession. Increases in the money supply can also overheat the economy—causing inflation

and thus introducing a new set of economic problems.

The government may also use fiscal policy—decreasing taxes, increasing spending, or both—in its efforts to stimulate a faltering economy. When the government increases spending (as it did in the buildup for World War II, for example), the demand for goods and services rises. This rise in demand increases employment and stimulates economic growth. Tax cuts are intended to work in a similar way: consumers who can keep an increased share of their income can presumably spend more. Fiscal policy changes may also fail, however. The necessary legislation may come too late to make a difference. New spending programs may be insufficient; tax cuts may be too small, or they may be targeted to benefit constituency groups for reasons unrelated to overall economic growth.

Government efforts to ensure economic stability and growth are also complicated by the degree to which national economies throughout the world have become interdependent. As world trade has increased, economic problems in one country can easily spread to others. For example, a nation in recession will be less able to purchase goods and services from other nations. The decrease in demand can cause job losses in other countries as producers of trade goods cut back. Similarly, economic shocks related to political instability or war can also have destructive ripple effects. In efforts to address international economic problems, many national governments now participate in cooperative efforts carried out through institutions like the International Monetary Fund and the World Bank.

Further Reading

Heilbroner, Robert. *The Worldly Philosophers: The Lives, Times and Ideas of the Great Economic Thinkers.* New York: Simon & Schuster, 1995.
Heilbroner, Robert, and Lester Thurow. *Economics Explained: Everything You Need to Know about How the Economy Works and Where It Is Going.* New York: Simon & Schuster, 1994.

—*David Long*

Recreation Industry

The recreation industry is a broad group of many different kinds of businesses that make money from what people do when they are not working. Of course, people fill their nonworking time with activities they have to do—buying groceries, tending to children, maintaining a home. Yet they also spend much time and money on activities they want to engage in—hobbies, sports, travel, concerts, and outdoor activities.

Recreation can be somewhat hard to define because some people do for fun what other people do for a living. A person might build a chair because carpentry is an enjoyable hobby or because that is what she is paid to do. Certain nonwork activities, for example, cooking or home improvement, can be essential activities in some contexts and recreational activities in others. A person slapping together a sandwich because he needs to eat is engaging in a different kind of activity than a person who carefully prepares a five-course gourmet meal for a dinner party of 20—all for no compensation apart from the satisfaction he gets from making a terrific meal.

People engage in many types of recreational activities—outdoor: camping, hiking, boating, hunting, and picnics; social and participatory: sports and games; cultural: concerts, movies, and museums; and communal: amusement parks and sporting events. At home, people engage in crafts like sewing, painting, jewelry making, and home decor. People also make models, garden, collect all sorts of items, and play video games.

This variety of activity makes the boundaries of the recreation industry difficult to set. Without question, the industry overlaps several others, just as recreational activities overlap other kinds of activities. The travel industry might seem to be part of the recreation industry—cruise ships, for instance, are certainly recreational—but many people must travel for their work, so

See also:
Arts and Entertainment Industry; Sports Industry; Tourism Industry.

To some people, preparing a big meal is a form of recreation.

Decorating is considered part of the recreation industry when people do it themselves.

sell travel services or provide recreation-dependent media, for example, Martha Stewart's craft-oriented magazines, television shows, and books.

Some of the largest direct providers of recreation, especially outdoor recreation, are the various levels of government. States, counties, and municipalities run many thousands of parks and recreation areas. The federal government also operates an extensive network of more than 300 parks, historic sites, and recreation areas that attract hundreds of millions of visitors every year. Many of the sites serve a dual purpose, and their recreational role at times conflicts with their other role. For example, national parks, seashores, and lakeshores were established in part to help protect wildlife and preserve ecosystems. Large numbers of visitors bring pollution and foot traffic that can cause environmental damage, so many of the more popular parks have had to take steps like restricting access to certain areas to minimize damage.

Nonprofits are also major providers of recreation. The Boy Scouts and Girl Scouts of America have long introduced children to camping, boating, and crafts. Community centers, which are often targeted to the elderly or children, provide recreation in an urban setting. In addition to religious services, churches and other houses of worship often provide recreational activities like bingo or dancing.

As entrepreneurs from Martha Stewart to Walt Disney have demonstrated, the recreation industry can also be quite profitable. The relatively high wages of American workers allow them the time and money to spend on recreational activities. Workers in the United States achieved more leisure time as the twentieth century progressed and the workweek shrank from 60 hours in 1900 to 40 or 35 by mid-century. Depending on how recreation is defined, anywhere from 7 to 14 percent of the average American's spending is on recreational activities, and that spending level tends to stay steady except during a war or a severe economic recession.

not all travel qualifies as recreation. The Home Depot and Lowe's chains of home-improvement stores sell to both hobbyists and building professionals. Food stores are not generally considered to be part of the recreation industry, but the Food Network cable television channel often is.

Some observers have attempted to impose some order on the industry by distinguishing between companies directly involved in the recreation industry and those indirectly involved. Companies that provide recreation directly would include businesses that run resorts and campsites. Indirect participants include companies that

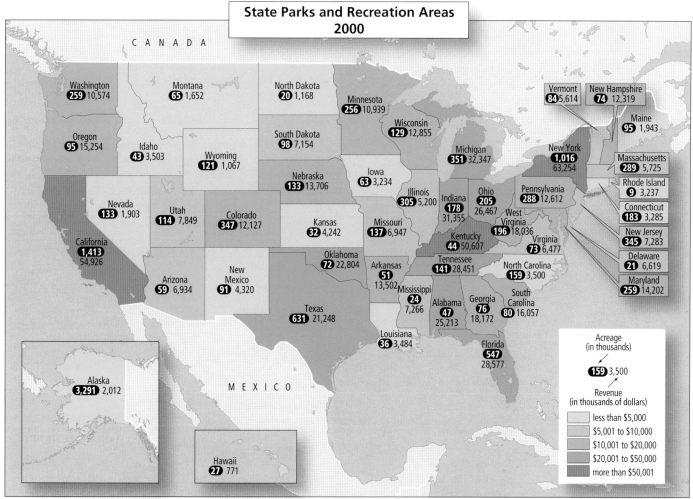

State Parks and Recreation Areas 2000

CANADA

Washington **259** 10,574

Montana **65** 1,652

North Dakota **20** 1,168

Minnesota **256** 10,939

Vermont **84** 5,614

New Hampshire **74** 12,319

Maine **95** 1,943

Oregon **95** 15,254

Idaho **43** 3,503

Wyoming **121** 1,067

South Dakota **98** 7,154

Wisconsin **129** 12,855

Michigan **351** 32,347

New York **1,016** 63,254

Massachusetts **289** 5,725

Rhode Island **9** 3,237

Nevada **133** 1,903

Utah **114** 7,849

Colorado **347** 12,127

Nebraska **133** 13,706

Iowa **63** 3,234

Illinois **305** 5,200

Indiana **178** 31,355

Ohio **205** 26,467

Pennsylvania **288** 12,612

West Virginia **196** 18,036

Connecticut **183** 3,285

New Jersey **345** 7,283

California **1,413** 54,926

Arizona **59** 6,934

New Mexico **91** 4,320

Kansas **32** 4,242

Missouri **137** 6,947

Kentucky **44** 50,607

Virginia **73** 6,477

Delaware **21** 6,619

Maryland **259** 14,202

Oklahoma **72** 22,804

Arkansas **51** 13,502

Tennessee **141** 28,451

North Carolina **159** 3,500

Texas **631** 21,248

Mississippi **24** 7,266

Alabama **47** 25,213

Georgia **76** 18,172

South Carolina **80** 16,057

Louisiana **36** 3,484

Florida **547** 28,577

MEXICO

Alaska **3,291** 2,012

Hawaii **27** 771

Acreage (in thousands)

159 3,500

Revenue (in thousands of dollars)

less than $5,000
$5,001 to $10,000
$10,001 to $20,000
$20,001 to $50,000
more than $50,001

Source: U.S. Bureau of the Census, "State Parks and Recreation Areas by State: 2000," *Statistical Abstracts of the United States,* 2001.

Being a part of the recreation industry is no guarantee of steady revenues, however. Although overall spending on recreation tends to stay constant, it can vary widely for any given kind of recreation. For example, after the terrorist attacks of September 11, 2001, consumer spending on travel and tourism declined sharply. However, consumer spending on home improvement increased as people spent more time making the place where they lived safer, nicer, and more comfortable. Likewise, the kinds of recreation chosen vary over a person's lifetime, even as spending stays relatively constant. New recreation technologies tend to steal market share from older forms; for example, cable television, home video games, and the Internet have siphoned off viewers from broadcast television.

Should recreational activities be discouraged because people engaging in recreational activities, while spending, are not working productively? To a degree, recreation is discouraged in the United States, especially when compared with Western Europe. The average European worker, for example, gets about three times as many days of paid vacation than does the average U.S. worker. Defenders of the U.S. system note that Americans also have higher levels of income than Europeans and suggest that working more and playing less benefits the overall economy.

On an individual level, however, working too many hours can drag down productivity because people get tired. Indeed, recreation offers many social benefits, which is one reason for government and nonprofit involvement in the industry. Recreation provides people with an opportunity to relax and recharge and to enjoy the fruits of their labors. It also gives people a chance to socialize and feel like they are part of a community.

Aside from providing enjoyment, the recreation industry is valuable because it helps people to relax with family and friends, which is good for productivity in the long run.

Just as the boundaries of the recreation industry are hard to draw, recreation's benefits are not tightly contained but spill over into all aspects of society.

Careers in the Recreation Industry

Because the recreation industry overlaps so many other industries, no one career path will lead to work in the industry. One person might train as a biologist and work at a national park, while another might train as a golfer and give classes at a local driving range.

In addition to encompassing many kinds of businesses, the recreation industry also offers many ways of working. Nonprofit and government recreation providers often rely on volunteer labor. Seasonal work is common in the recreation industry with many amusement parks, campgrounds, and swimming pools being open only in the summer. Part-time work is also common. As a result, the recreation industry is a major employer of students and seniors who are not seeking full-time, year-round jobs. No business could last long without full-time, year-round managers. For professionals in the recreation industry, a major challenge is to find seasonal workers and integrate the schedules of various part-timers as well as any volunteers.

Although qualifications and time commitment may vary, one necessary component for work in the recreation industry is the appropriate attitude and good social skills. The specific activity may vary from one recreation business to the next, but the customers are all there for one reason: to enjoy themselves.

Further Reading

Crossley, John C., and Lynn M. Jamieson. *Introduction to Commercial and Entrepreneurial Recreation.* Champaign, Ill.: Sagamore Publishing, 1997.

Goodale, Thomas L., and Geoffrey C. Godbey. *The Evolution of Leisure: Historical and Philosophical Perspectives.* State College, Pa.: Venture Publishing, 1988.

Goodale, Thomas L., and Peter A. Witt, eds. *Recreation and Leisure: Issues in an Era of Change.* 3rd ed. State College, Pa.: Venture Publishing, 1991.

Kelly, John R. *Recreation Business.* New York: John Wiley & Sons, 1985.

Loomis, John B., and Richard G. Walsh. *Recreation Economic Decisions: Comparing Benefits and Costs.* State College, Pa.: Venture Publishing, 1997.

—*Mary Sisson*

Regulation of Business and Industry

In a market economy such as exists in the United States, price should ideally act as the information, incentive, and rationing mechanism that determines supply and demand. In practice, however, the operations of markets are not perfect. In addition, economies of scale and extraordinary capital requirements have resulted in the development of natural monopolies that dominate business in areas like public transportation, telecommunications, and power. Given the existence of market imperfections and of monopoly power, free markets alone cannot guarantee equitable distribution of resources in a complex industrial society. As a consequence, U.S. governments have established regulatory bodies to promote fair trade practices and to safeguard citizens.

The U.S. Congress, state legislatures, and local governments have all created commissions empowered to establish and enforce standards for specific activities in the private sector. Members of regulatory agencies are generally appointed by the executive branch of government and serve for fixed terms. The commissions are empowered to impose regulations that have the force of law. They may also conduct hearings and rule on whether their regulations are being followed.

Railroad Regulation

Railroads were the first big businesses in the United States. Rapid expansion between 1860 and 1880, however, resulted in excess railroad capacity. As a consequence, railroads attempted to maximize their returns by adopting a number of discriminatory price practices. Outraged by unfair treatment, in the early 1870s farmers and other businesses successfully pressured several midwestern states to pass regulatory laws that established commissions to set maximum rates, prohibited charging exorbitant rates

for short hauls, and generally made illegal price discrimination based on the identity of the shipper or place of shipment. The U.S. Supreme Court in *Munn v. Illinois* (1877) upheld a state's right to regulate railroads and other businesses "clothed with a public interest" within its boundaries. In *Wabash, St. Louis and Pacific Railway Company v. Illinois* (1886), the Court, however, ruled that the efforts of Illinois to regulate rates between states infringed on the federal government's exclusive control of interstate commerce.

In 1887 Congress passed the Act to Regulate Commerce, which brought all railroads engaged in interstate commerce under federal regulation. The act also established the Interstate Commerce Commission (ICC), the first permanent federal regulatory agency. The five-member ICC was empowered to oversee the management of the railroads, hear complaints stemming from violations of the act, and require railroads to file annual reports using uniform accounting practices.

The ICC was the prototype for later federal regulatory agencies. Like its precursors at the state level, it was composed of members with specialized knowledge of the railroads. Permanent and independent, the ICC gained recognition as an impartial and non-partisan body capable of equitable regulation. The Hepburn Act of 1906 increased the membership of the ICC from five to seven and empowered the commission to fix just and reasonable maximum rail rates, to establish uniform accounting methods, and broaden the commission's jurisdiction to

See also:
Deregulation; Environmental Regulation; Federal Trade Commission; Securities and Exchange Commission; Sherman Antitrust Act.

Interstate Commerce Commission 1887 to 1995	
Mandate: Regulate surface transportation, including • railroads • trucking companies • bus lines • freight forwarders • water carriers • oil pipelines • transportation brokers • express agencies	**Powers:** • set rates • investigate rate issues • establish uniform accounting methods • consolidate railroad systems • manage labor disputes in interstate transport • enforce desegregation of passenger terminal facilities

U.S. Courts and Restraint of Trade	
Era	Court Position
1880s to late 1930s	Courts follow "rule of reason." Restriction of competition is not unlawful if it does not involve predatory practices.
Late 1930s to 1970s	Control of a large market share considered to be per se illegal.
1970s to 2000s	Courts focus on the degree of competition rather than the number of firms in an industry.

include sleeping-car companies, ferries, oil pipelines, terminals, and bridges.

Antitrust Regulation

In the last decades of the nineteenth century, fear of monopoly power and the abuse that was associated with the consolidation of many industries, most notably the monopolistic behavior of Standard Oil, led to passage of the Sherman Antitrust Act in 1890. The act outlawed "every contract, combination in the form of trust or otherwise, or conspiracy in restraint of trade." In 1914 Congress approved the Federal Trade Commission Act to further advance the government's efforts to prevent unfair methods of competition in interstate commerce. The act established the five-member, bipartisan Federal Trade Commission (FTC). The FTC was charged with collecting annual and special reports from corporations; these reports were and are used to assess industry concentration and impact on competition. The FTC was also authorized to investigate charges of unfair business practices including misbranding and misleading advertising, to publish its findings, and to issue cease and desist orders in cases where illegal practices were found to exist.

Establishment of the FTC acknowledged that industrial growth demanded a complex system of government regulation, but until the late 1930s the courts followed the "rule of reason" with respect to restraint of trade. That is, courts held that restriction of competition was not unlawful if it did not involve predatory practices like collusion among independent firms. Given this narrow legal interpretation, large size alone was insufficient for a finding of violation of antitrust laws.

After 1938, however, the Justice Department and courts began to rule that control of a large market share was per se illegal, and prosecutions of antitrust cases dramatically increased. The government won most of these cases, but the courts imposed relatively minor penalties. In the 1970s the courts moved away from per se interpretation of the law, focusing on the degree of competition rather than the number of firms in an industry. This shift in interpretation was at least partly responsible for the government's dropping its case against IBM in 1982. The recognition of the importance of global competition led the Justice Department to approve the Boeing Aircraft Corporation's acquisition of its major domestic competitor, McDonnell Douglass, in 1997. The prosecution of Microsoft in the late 1990s involved issues of both predatory behavior and stifling of competition, but even in that case, the initial ruling that called for the company's breakup was reversed.

During the 1920s the FTC's role in safeguarding consumers against deceptive sales practices became well established, and, by the early 1930s, more than 90 percent of the complaints issued by the agency involved issues of consumer deception. The FTC is authorized to impose a variety of remedies, including affirmative disclosure that provides additional information about an advertised product; corrective advertising that requires a firm to sponsor additional advertising to correct the effects of its previous misleading ads; and restitution or refunds to consumers who have been misled by deceptive advertising.

The New Deal

The Great Depression of the 1930s called into question the efficacy of the free market system. With the U.S. economy on the brink of collapse, President Franklin D. Roosevelt between 1933 and 1938 sponsored legislation that began or expanded federal regulation of many aspects of business. Roosevelt's New Deal included the Emergency Banking Relief Act (1933), which provided for government supervision of U.S. banks, while the

Glass–Steagall Act (1933) separated commercial and investment banking functions and insured bank deposits through the Federal Deposit Insurance Corporation. The Securities Exchange Act (1934) established the Securities and Exchange Commission (SEC) and required the registration and disclosure of information concerning securities traded on exchanges. The Federal Communications Commission (1934) was created to regulate communications by telegraph, cable, and radio, while the Federal Housing Administration (1934) came into existence to insure loans for new home construction and for repairs to existing housing.

To aid farmers, the New Deal effectively removed agriculture from the free market by creating a system of acreage allotments and price supports. To assist industrial workers, the New Deal created the National Labor Relations Board (1935) to oversee negotiations between management and labor. The Motor Carrier Act (1935) put buses and trucks engaged in interstate commerce under the control of the ICC. The Public Utility Holding Company Act (1935) gave the Federal Power Commission authority to regulate interstate transmission of electric power, gave the FTC authority over interstate transmission of gas, and gave the SEC jurisdiction over the financial practices of utility holding companies. The Merchant Marine Act (1936) created the U.S. Maritime Commission to develop the American merchant marine, and the Wagner–Steagall Act (1936) created the U.S. Housing Authority to assist in the development of low-rent housing. The Food, Drug, and Cosmetic Act (1938) extended the FTC's control over the advertising of food, drugs, and cosmetics, and the Civil Aeronautics Act (1938) created the Civil Aeronautics Authority to regulate air transport rates and assure the stability of the air transport industry.

The proliferation of federal agencies during the New Deal reflected confidence in the ability of expert commissions to provide the most equitable oversight of the economy. In his book *The Administrative Process* (1938), James Landis, a former member of the SEC, best articulated the rationale for administrative regulation. He argued that the executive,

On March 9, 1933, President Franklin Roosevelt signs the Emergency Banking Relief Act.

Regulation of Business and Industry

1870s
Several midwestern states pass regulatory laws to outlaw price discrimination by railroads.

1877
In *Munn v. Illinois* the U.S. Supreme Court upholds a state's right to regulate railroads.

1887
Act to Regulate Commerce passed.

1890
Sherman Antitrust Act passed.

1906
Hepburn Act passed.

1907
Wisconsin and New York become the first states to establish public service commissions to oversee public utilities.

1914
Federal Trade Commission Act passed.

1933 to 1938
Many regulatory laws and agencies established as part of the New Deal: Emergency Banking Relief Act (1933), Glass–Steagall Act (1933), Securities Exchange Act (1934), Federal Communications Commission (1934), Federal Housing Administration (1934), National Labor Relations Board (1935), Motor Carrier Act (1935), Public Utility Holding Company Act (1935), Merchant Marine Act (1936), Wagner–Steagall Act (1936), Food, Drug, and Cosmetic Act (1938), and Civil Aeronautics Act (1938).

1964 to 1975
Regulatory agencies established: Equal Employment Opportunity Commission (1964), National Transportation Safety Board (1966), Council on Environmental Quality (1969), Environmental Protection Agency (1970), National Highway Traffic Safety Administration (1970), Occupational Safety and Health Administration (1970), Consumer Product Safety Commission (1972), Mining Enforcement and Safety Administration (1973), and Materials Transportation Bureau (1975).

1974
Economist Alfred Kahn establishes basis for deregulation of some industries.

1978
The U.S. Airline Deregulation Act passed.

1982
The U.S. government drops its antitrust case against IBM.

1997
Justice Department approves Boeing Aircraft's acquisition of its major domestic competitor, McDonnell Douglass.

2001
Decision to break up Microsoft reversed.

legislative, and judicial branches of government were ill prepared to address complex, modern issues; in contrast, regulators possessed expertise that was developed "only from that continuity of interest, that ability and desire to devote 52 weeks a year, year after year, to a particular problem."

Social Regulation

The first wave of regulatory activity in the United States focused on maintaining competition in an era of business consolidation; the second arose from the market failures associated with the Great Depression. The third wave of regulation was directed at protecting consumers, employees, and the general public interest from corporate harm. These latest efforts gave the government oversight of many of the most important areas of corporate decision making, including hiring, employee work conditions, product safety standards, and pollution control. They have also had a major impact on virtually all industries.

Between 1964 and 1977 Congress created 10 federal regulatory agencies: the Equal Employment Opportunity Commission (1964), the National Transportation Safety Board (1966), the Council on Environmental Quality (1969), the Environmental Protection Agency (1970), the National Highway Traffic Safety Administration (1970), the Occupational Safety and Heath Administration (1970), the Consumer Product Safety Commission (1972), the Mining Enforcement and Safety Administration (1973), the Materials Transportation Bureau (1975), and the Office of Strip Mining Regulation and Enforcement (1977). These agencies greatly enlarged the size of the federal government and substantially raised government expenditures as well as business costs related to compliance with regulatory mandates.

Regulatory efforts during the 1960s and 1970s brought business and nonbusiness interests into sharp opposition. Earlier regulatory eras often found business working with government in shaping regulatory legislation. In the 1960s and 1970s, by contrast, civil rights activists, consumer groups, and environmental protection advocates joined with other public interest organizations to lobby for regulatory legislation, and, in many cases, business was left out of the process of administrative policy formulation.

State Regulation

The term *public utility* is used to identify a range of industries that provide services like transportation, communication, electrical power, gas, and water that are used by the general citizenry. Although utilities are typically private, investor-owned firms, competition does not characterize these markets. Instead, the importance of economies of scale and a desire to take advantage of those efficiencies led to the emergence of natural monopolies—only one provider of a specific

Eras of Regulatory Activity		
Era	Regulatory Focus	Business Role
1880s to 1930s	• Maintaining competition	Business works with government in shaping regulation.
1930s to 1960s	• Correcting market failures • Using expert commissions to provide equitable oversight of the economy	
1960s to 1970s	• Protecting consumers, employees, and general public from corporate harm	Business is often left out of the process of policy formulation.
1980s to 2000s	• Deregulating key industries, including transportation, banking, and telecommunications • Enforcing social and environmental regulation	

Estimated Annual Costs and Benefits of Federal Regulation
April 1995 to September 2001
(in millions of 2001 dollars)

Federal Agency	Estimated Annual Costs	Estimated Annual Benefits
Agriculture	2,249 to 2,271	2,938 to 5,989
Education	362 to 610	655 to 814
Department of Energy	1,836	3,991 to 4,059
Health and Human Services	2,988 to 3,067	8165 to 9,182
Housing and Urban Development	150	190
Department of Labor	361	1,173 to 3,557
Department of Transportation	1,756 to 3,808	2,400 to 4,312
Environmental Protection Agency	41,523 to 42,326	29,140 to 66,092
Total	51,225 to 54,429	48,652 to 67,602

Source: *Federal Register* 67, no. 60, March 28, 2002.

Quantifying the amount spent on and the amount saved by federal regulation can be difficult. Such estimates are important, however, in assessing whether the regulation is useful. (Agencies use different methods for assessing expenditures and savings— thus the great variance in the estimates provided.)

service in a given area—as the earliest electrical power, gas, water, and telephone utilities developed in the United States.

Local and state governments acknowledged efficiencies associated with a single, large utility provider, but they also recognized the need to protect consumers from abuses associated with monopoly power. In 1907 Wisconsin and New York became the first states to establish public service commissions to oversee public utilities; by 1913 nearly all the other states had followed their example. The state commissions were charged with

assuring that the operation of utilities conformed to the public interest with regard to pricing and provision of service.

Given the charge to oversee rates and to determine conditions of service, regulators have often been involved with decisions that in other kinds of firms are under the control of management. This circumstance produced conflict as early as the 1920s in relation to issues like the fair value of the property owned by utilities, equitable returns for utility stockholders, and reasonable utility rates. From the 1920s until the late 1960s, however, technological innovation and increasing economies of scale produced a situation where consumers benefited from declining rates in many regulated industries, while investors in those utilities enjoyed increasing returns.

After 1970 utilities, particularly those providing electric power, faced new challenges as technological improvements slowed, fuel charges rose, and demands for costly environmental safeguards increased. Utilities applied for rate increases, but state commissions, many of which were staffed by lawyers, tended to ignore economic considerations. In 1974, however, economist Alfred Kahn became chairman of the New York Public Service Commission. Arguing that "applied microeconomics is the exciting new frontier of public policy," Kahn encouraged the New York commission to employ economic analysis

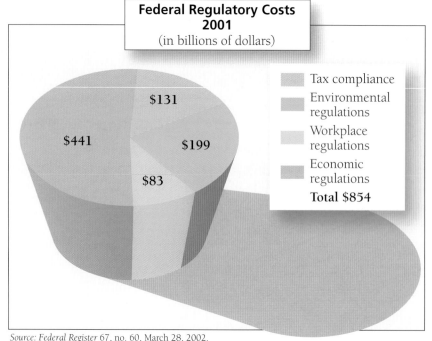

Federal Regulatory Costs
2001
(in billions of dollars)

$131
$441
$199
$83

Tax compliance
Environmental regulations
Workplace regulations
Economic regulations
Total $854

Source: *Federal Register* 67, no. 60, March 28, 2002.

in its regulatory efforts. This analysis led New York state to introduce a new rate structure for electric power that took into account the actual costs of serving business and residential customers. It also led New York to unbundle telephone charges so that consumers would not subsidize business customers or pay for services like directory assistance if they did not use them.

Kahn's work in New York gained national attention. Many other state agencies copied his pricing structures. Even more important, the use of economic analysis, which Kahn helped promote, had the long-term effect of suggesting, during the decades that followed, the need to deregulate some industries.

Deregulation

The administration of President Jimmy Carter took up the banner of deregulation. Carter believed that excessive regulation inhibited efficiency in many industries, and he accepted the argument that regulatory agencies had often been captured by the interests they had been designed to control. Among the industries he identified for deregulation were the airlines, trucking, and railroads; in addition, he supported decontrol of natural gas prices.

In 1978 Congress passed the United States Airline Deregulation Act. The act abolished the Civil Aeronautics Board, left airlines free to establish rates and routes, and opened the industry to new entrants. The act is noteworthy because it reversed a century-long trend of increasing government intervention in the economy. Two years later, the Motor Carrier Act began the deregulation of interstate trucking by giving firms greater control over rates and by making it easier for new businesses to enter the industry. Also in 1980 the Staggers Rail Act curtailed the ICC's powers to set rail rates. (The ICC was disbanded in 1995.) Carter's deregulation strategies were essentially pragmatic; the trend toward greater deregulation and increased limits on regulatory agencies would intensify and become more ideological during the administration of Ronald Reagan, who was elected in 1980.

During a press conference in 2000, U.S. Consumer Product Safety Commission chairwoman Ann Brown demonstrates how the seat of the Option 5 High Chairs separates from the frame, allowing the child to fall to the ground. Retailer Costco recalled about one million of the chairs after receiving 57 reports of injuries.

The last decades of the twentieth century witnessed two divergent trends in regulation of business and industry. The introduction of new kinds of competitors into industries long considered to be natural monopolies promoted deregulation of the transportation, banking, and telecommunications industries. The social and environmental regulation initiated in the 1960s and 1970s remains in force and appears likely to have a lasting impact on the relationship between business interests and those of the larger society.

Further Reading

Kolko, Gabriel. *Railroads and Regulation, 1877–1916.* Princeton, N.J.: Princeton University Press, 1965.

Leuchtenberg, William E. *Franklin D. Roosevelt and the New Deal, 1932–1940.* New York: Harper & Row, 1963.

McCraw, Thomas K. *Prophets of Regulation.* Cambridge, Mass.: Belknap Press of Harvard University Press, 1984.

Stone, Alan. *Economic Regulation and the Public Interest: The Federal Trade Commission in Theory and Practice.* Ithaca, N.Y.: Cornell University Press, 1977.

—*Marilyn Lavin*

Research and Development

Research takes an idea and turns it into a prototype or new process. Development takes the prototype and unproven process and makes them a reality. Research and development (R&D) are as old as fire: people saw fire and what it could do, then learned to control it for their own purposes. That same desire to know and understand drives R&D today—to improve the human condition and to prosper from it.

Early R&D

Combining research and development puts science and business under one umbrella. In nineteenth-century America science education was usually sought overseas, thus the country had few available scientists. Late in the century, U.S. universities began adding science and engineering programs. Graduates of these programs, coupled with increased commercial competition because of the new American antitrust laws, promoted the combining of research and development. In 1932 Irving Langmuir became the first American corporate researcher to win the Nobel Prize in economics.

In the early 1950s Robert Solow of the Massachusetts Institute of Technology (Nobel Prize in economics, 1987) demonstrated mathematically that the gross national product per worker is tied more closely to technological progress (the

Year	Sources of funds (in millions of dollars)				Objective (percent of total)		
	Federal government	Industry	Universities/ colleges	Nonprofit	Defense-related[1]	Space-related[2]	Other
1960	8,915	4,516	67	123	53	3	44
1962	10,138	5,124	84	179	49	7	45
1964	12,764	5,888	114	200	37	19	43
1966	14,165	7,331	165	252	32	20	47
1968	14,964	9,008	221	290	35	14	52
1970	14,984	10,449	259	343	33	10	56
1972	16,039	11,715	312	393	33	8	59
1974	17,287	14,885	393	474	29	7	64
1976	20,292	17,702	480	592	27	8	66
1978	24,468	22,457	679	727	26	6	69
1980	30,035	30,929	920	871	24	5	71
1982	37,233	40,692	1,207	1,095	26	5	68
1984	46,571	52,187	1,514	1,351	29	3	67
1986	54,711	60,991	2,019	1,647	32	3	65
1988	60,180	67,977	2,527	2,081	30	3	66
1990	61,669	83,208	3,187	2,589	25	4	70
1992	60,923	96,229	3,568	3,113	22	4	74
1994	60,790	99,203	3,936	3,664	20	4	76
1996	63,392	123,412	4,430	4,238	18	4	78
1998	66,827	147,867	5,183	5,007	16	4	81
2000[3]	69,627	181,040	5,969	5,789	14	3	83

R&D Expenditures 1960 to 2000

[1]R&D spending by the Department of Defense, including space activities, and a portion of the Department of Energy funds
[2]For the National Aeronautics and Space Administration only [3]Preliminary
Source: U.S. National Science Foundation, *National Patterns of R&D Resources,* annual.

product of R&D) than to capital investment. Companies subsequently began to funnel many resources to research and development. The R&D powerhouses were typically major players in their market: Bell Laboratories, General Electric, and later IBM, Xerox, and Hewlett-Packard. These immensely wealthy firms funded the research that won many of their scientists Nobel Prizes.

By the late 1980s large corporations were feeling the pinch of global competition; overseas businesses were bringing products to market in shorter cycles. Many of corporate America's R&D departments had to reinvent themselves to keep up with the competition; they radically changed everything from how they approached a research topic to their involvement in the manufacturing and distribution processes.

Contemporary R&D

R&D has experienced a general move from stand-alone inventions to integrated innovations. The Internet is an example of R&D that requires integrated solutions. Researchers must understand, or at least take into account, the areas of voice, data, networking, software, hardware, communications systems, and related peripherals to create a product that takes advantage of what the Internet offers.

In the past, one major breakthrough could give the parent company a significant marketing edge or start a revolution in its field. Currently, a lot of small inventions are usually combined to make a revolution. In the 1990s R&D departments acknowledged this shift and changed their fundamental operation within the company. Because major breakthroughs no longer assured a corporation major profits, much research was curtailed or stopped completely. Companies began concentrating on short-term applied research. Goals were tied more closely to the corporation's profits. Instead of looking for breakthroughs worthy of the Nobel Prize, R&D began developing small improvements to existing products.

Trends in Corporate Funds for Industrial Research and Development 1960 to 1999
(in constant 1996 millions of dollars)

Year	Basic Research	Applied Research	Development	Total
1960	1,338	5,390	13,227	19,955
1961	1,399	5,192	14,211	20,802
1962	1,517	6,324	14,274	22,115
1963	1,630	6,304	15,370	23,304
1964	1,645	6,684	16,487	24,816
1965	1,707	6,812	18,583	27,103
1966	1,844	7,375	20,282	29,501
1967	1,694	7,334	22,785	31,813
1968	1,757	7,913	24,053	33,722
1969	1,660	8,235	25,832	35,727
1970	1,528	8,183	25,692	35,403
1971	1,494	7,998	25,416	34,908
1972	1,455	8,052	26,744	36,251
1973	1,485	8,429	29,086	39,000
1974	1,464	8,910	29,678	40,052
1975	1,431	8,594	28,901	38,926
1976	1,499	9,248	30,473	1,220
1977	1,557	9,576	31,826	42,959
1978	1,628	10,097	34,128	45,853
1979	1,709	10,852	36,641	49,202
1980	1,815	11,483	40,131	53,429
1981	2,105	13,402	41,295	56,803
1982	2,299	14,133	44,104	60,536
1983	2,555	14,933	47,244	64,733
1984	2,984	16,155	52,815	71,954
1985	3,220	17,517	56,673	77,409
1986	4,642	20,027	54,912	79,580
1987	4,618	19,532	54,997	79,148
1988	4,372	20,610	58,140	83,122
1989	4,602	21,608	62,058	88,268
1990	4,346	21,306	68,674	94,327
1991	6,831	23,896	70,299	101,026
1992	6,333	23,066	73,372	102,774
1993	6,338	21,219	73,023	100,575
1994	6,331	20,177	74,662	101,168
1995	5,483	24,215	81,056	110,756
1996	6,848	25,370	88,798	121,015
1997	8,598	29,212	93,246	131,055
1998	11,336	26,941	102,215	140,492
1999	12,230	30,473	110,288	152,990

Source: National Science Foundation/Division of Science Resources Statistics, "Survey of Industrial Research and Development," 1999.

Previously, investing in research typically meant a great deal of money in the company's pocket from spectacular breakthroughs that

**Federal Funds for Industrial R&D by
Selected Federal Agencies**
(in millions of dollars)

	1997	1998	1999
Department of Defense	12,603	13,709	11,650
National Aeronautics and Space Administration	2,022	1,522	1,469
Department of Energy	2,505	1,998	2,209
All agencies	23,928	24,164	22,535

Source: National Science Foundation/Division of Science Resources Statistics,
"Survey of Industrial Research and Development," 1999.

gave them a tremendous competitive edge. With the R&D cycle greatly accelerated, some companies are making a lot of money from other company's inventions without investing in their own R&D departments. For example, computer companies like Dell and Compaq do not do much inventing—instead, they excel at the manufacture, marketing, and distribution pieces of the development equation, giving them a competitive edge without incurring the overhead costs of research.

A major issue in the field of research and development is that of protecting ideas and inventions. The United States has laws to protect inventions and innovations, but not ideas. Article 1, Section 8 of the U.S. Constitution gives Congress the right to offer protection to writers (copyrights) and inventors (patents) for a set time. Writers and inventors must apply for protection by registering the content of their original work. The goal is to offer exclusive rights in exchange for shared information; others can build on that knowledge but must pay for it.

Patents are granted for 20 years, then the information goes into the public domain. Anyone can then produce the invention, but they cannot re-patent the same idea. Three kinds of patents—utility patents, which document function or results of a process; design patents, which protect the ornamental look (rather than function) of an object; and plant patents, which protect plant combinations used for hybrids—are available in the United States. Patents may be licensed to others—the patent owner can allow someone else to develop the product and market it. The patent owner usually exchanges the patent rights for part of the profits.

In some cases, an inventor may not want to apply for a patent so as to preserve the uniqueness of his or her invention. For example, documenting a special recipe or production process would give competitors the ability to reproduce those results. Instead, the developer is bound by a trade-secret agreement not to reveal the unique aspect of the invention.

Although corporations are now major players in research and development, many individual inventors contributed to American industry, from Alexander Graham Bell to Tim Berners-Lee, inventor of the World Wide Web. These inventors and others like them had the drive to see their ideas become a reality. However, their greatest common attribute is probably persistence. The inventor Thomas Edison, who held 1,093 patents, once said, "I failed my way to success."

Further Reading

Buderi, Robert. *Engines of Tomorrow: How the World's Best Companies Are Using Their Research Labs to Win the Future.* New York: Simon & Schuster, 2000.

Cohen, Linda R., and Roger G. Noll. *Research and Development after the Cold War.* Stanford, Calif.: Center for Economic Policy Research, Stanford University, 1995.

Corben, Herbert C. *The Struggle to Understand: A History of Human Wonder and Discovery.* New York: Prometheus Books, 1991.

Kanbar, Maurice. *Secrets from an Inventor's Notebook.* San Francisco: Council Oaks Books, 2001.

—*Stephanie Buckwalter*

Resume

A resume is a communication between a job hunter and a potential employer. It is more than a job history or a list of skills, abilities, and education. A resume is a piece of persuasive writing—a word picture describing the package offered by the potential employee. Because it describes a package, a resume should include hard skills, soft skills, education, professional or academic recognition, and measurable accomplishments.

Hard skills are measurable and easily demonstrated, for example, typing 80 words per minute, programming in various computer languages, vehicle repair, or bookkeeping. Soft skills include adept management of people and leadership. Such skills are not directly measurable except through observation over time. Developing soft skills and documenting them on a resume is particularly important for those in, or wishing to be in, management. Even seemingly minor jobs can be redeemed on a resume. For example, a student who has refereed basketball games can add "ability to make split-second decisions under pressure." A food-service worker can report "learned excellent communication skills through public contact." Statements like these tell potential employers that the person sees the bigger picture.

Business is driven by results. A successful resume will highlight measurable accomplishments and quantifiable results. Any time prospective employees can show where their participation has added to an employer's bottom line, they will increase their chances of future employment. Quantifiable results are, for instance, "increased sales in my region by 15 percent in one year," "wrote business proposals that brought in three new clients," "streamlined distribution, cutting costs by $1,000 per quarter," and so on. Even small improvements that affect the bottom line make a big difference.

Resumes are of two general kinds. The first, and most common, is the chronological resume. This kind of resume lists all jobs in reverse chronological order, with the most recent mentioned first. Each job is described in terms of experience and skills mastered—both hard and soft skills. Quantifiable results should also be included.

The other kind of resume is a functional resume. Instead of listing jobs chronologically, experience is listed according to function. This kind of resume is helpful for those who have gaps in their work history or possibly for someone starting out on a new career track with lots of experience scattered throughout various activities, volunteer opportunities, coursework, and unrelated jobs. For example, a person may have three years of marketing experience but not in one place. Instead, the experience comes from a marketing survey project from

See also:
Human Resources;
Job Search.

Sample Chronological Resume

Claudia Perez
13234 Olive Dr.
Houston, Texas 00000
555-0445
Claudia_Perez@yahoo.com

Summary
Book production assistant with strengths in computer-based production, online product development, and four-color printing.

Experience

Encyclopedic Books, Inc.   **2001 to present**
Reference publisher for academic market

   Assistant, Production Department

   Key Accomplishments
   • Participated in production of approximately 60 print and electronic titles annually
   • Created in-house database of all back-list titles
   • Negotiated printing contracts cutting costs by 35%
   • Assisted with in-house production of computer-generated materials
   • Awarded maximum company bonus for performance

Enlightened Books, Inc.   **2000 to 2001**
Supplemental education publisher for secondary schools

   Intern

   Key Accomplishments
   • Organized production department
   • Created in-house photo research database

Skills
Microsoft Word
Microsoft Excel
Pagemaker

Education
Bachelor's degree, University of Texas
Microsoft certification

school, volunteering at the local Chamber of Commerce, and helping a friend get a business started. All of these would be grouped under the appropriate heading. A functional resume can raise a red flag for employers because some people who use this style are trying to hide something, either a spotty work history or job-hopping without a coherent plan.

Resumes are divided into sections. Some sections are optional, others are mandatory. All resumes should have the person's legal name and contact information: address, telephone numbers, and e-mail address. The next section, which is optional, is typically a one-sentence job objective or career summary. An objective is helpful if the experience listed does not meet the criteria for the job. A career summary is a great way to highlight major accomplishments or specific skills related to a targeted position, for example, a human resources professional with a specialty in COBRA administration.

Next comes experience. As noted above, this section can take a variety of forms. Regardless of the format, honesty and accuracy are required when describing previous job experience. Other sections include skills (for example, programming languages or platforms), and sometimes course work—especially if no related business experience can be shown—activities, honors, and professional memberships or affiliations. Another section

Elements of a Resume
• Hard skills
• Soft skills
• Education
• Professional or academic recognition
• Measurable accomplishments

is typically education. Education includes post–high school education, certifications, and training specific to the field. The last sections may be arranged in any order, depending upon what the applicant wants to highlight for the potential employer.

Many resumes include one or two references—names of people with whom the applicant has had a previous working relationship. Employers often contact references to discuss merits of prospective employees. Good references include former employers or supervisors. For students, a favorite teacher would also be an acceptable reference. (Ask the person if he or she is willing to serve as a reference before including him or her on the resume.)

Resumes should be specific. Generalizations do not help a potential employer make a hiring decision. Prospective employers look for specific skills, the person's potential to do the job well, past contributions to other employers, and the possible value added to their company. The more attractive the package presented on the resume, the more likely the applicant will be called for an interview.

Resumes have no hard and fast rules. They are quite flexible but come with one warning. Although a resume does not guarantee a person a particular job, a poorly crafted resume can lose the job.

The Cover Letter

A resume is a standardized document, but a cover letter allows a job applicant to tailor his or her submission to each company applied to. Cover letters give the opportunity to hear the individual voice of the applicant. The letter can reflect personality, special talents and abilities, and, perhaps most important, specific interest in the company. Before writing a cover letter, conduct sufficient research to ascertain what the goals and interests of a company are as well as its expectations of employees. An applicant's cover letter should reflect this knowledge of the company and of the particular job.

A cover letter should be addressed to the specific individual who will process the application. It should refer to the position for which one is applying and explain why the applicant is a strong and capable candidate. Although not in the same detail as a resume, a cover letter should highlight an individual's relevant accomplishments and achievements and should refer to the resume in some way as a reference for additional information. Finally, a cover letter should end with a request for a specific follow-up—an interview or phone call—and should state clearly the applicant's contact information.

Further Reading

Fry, Ronald W. *Your First Resume: For Students and Anyone Preparing to Enter Today's Tough Job Market.* 5th ed. Franklin Lakes, N.J.: Career Press, 2001.

Kennedy, Joyce Lane. *Resumes for Dummies.* 3rd ed. New York: John Wiley & Sons, 2000.

Yate, Martin John. *Resumes That Knock 'Em Dead,* 4th ed. Holbrook, Mass.: Adams Media, 2000.

—*Stephanie Buckwalter*

Retail and Wholesale

Retailers and wholesalers are market intermediaries: retailers make physical products and services available to consumers; wholesalers facilitate the flow of goods from producers to other businesses. The functions performed by retailers and wholesalers contribute value to consumer goods and services. This added value justifies the additional costs associated with retailers' and wholesalers' participation in the distribution channels that extend from manufacturers to final customers.

The North American Industry Classification System (NAICS), adopted jointly by Canada, Mexico, and the United States in 1997, defines the boundaries between wholesale and retail trade. The classification is based on the method of business operation; this determination is a change from the previous Standard Industrial Classification (SIC), which had defined wholesale and retail on the basis of kind of customer served. According to NAICS typology, the wholesale sector is composed of businesses that "sell goods in large quantities using business-oriented methods like specialized catalogs, customer contacts, and warehouse or office locations." The NAICS Retail Trade, Accommodation, and Food Service sector is an expansion of the SIC Retail Trade division. It includes businesses that "sell merchandise in small quantities using public-oriented methods like mass media advertising, high-traffic locations, and attractive displays."

Retailers: Who They Are and What They Do
Retailing is a broad field and is not limited to stores. It includes sellers who reach customers through such varied means as direct response, television shopping channels, the Internet, catalogs, and vending machines. Moreover, retailers provide services as well as goods. Theme parks, banks, restaurants, stockbrokers, and child care providers are considered to be retail service firms.

Retailing traces its origins to the itinerant peddlers and town marketplaces that for centuries made possible the exchange of goods. Although peddlers and markets continue to provide this service in many parts of the world, the appearance of permanent stores and business districts in many European cities during the Renaissance marked an important step in the development of retail practice. For many centuries, retail chains existed in China; during the fifteenth and sixteenth centuries, the Fugger family operated a mercantile chain in Germany. However, the Great Atlantic and Pacific Tea Company (A&P), which was founded in New York City in 1859, is considered to be the first modern chain store.

As early as the seventeenth century, department-type stores were present in Europe and Asia; during the mid-nineteenth century, Bon Marché developed into a full-scale department store in Paris. At about the same time, R. H. Macy's and Marshall Field's were founded in the United States.

See also:
Consumerism; Distribution Channels; E-Business; Franchise; Globalization; NAICS Codes.

Retail Trade Sales: 1980 to 2000

Year	Total (billion dollars)	Annual percent change[1]	Per capita[2] (dollars)
1980	957	6.8	4,213
1985	1,375	6.8	5,779
1989	1,759	6.2	7,127
1990	1,845	4.9	7,394
1991	1,856	0.6	7,360
1992	1,952	5.2	7,652
1993	2,082	6.7	8,077
1994	2,248	8.0	8,636
1995	2,359	4.9	8,976
1996	2,502	6.1	9,435
1997	2,611	4.4	9,749
1998	2,746	5.2	10,160
1999	2,995	9.1	10,983
2000	3,061	2.2	11,254

[1] Change from immediate prior year [2] Based on Census Bureau estimates of resident population as of July 1
Source: U.S. Bureau of the Census, Current Business Reports, Annual Benchmark Report for Retail Trade, Washington, D.C., January 1990–December 1999, BR/99-A and prior issues; and unpublished data, Washington, D.C.

Shopping Centers: 1990 to 2001

(number and retail sales by gross leasable area)

Year	Total	Gross leasable area (sq. ft.)					
		Less than 100,000	100,001- 200,000	200,001- 400,000	400,001- 800,000	800,001- 1,000,000	More than 1 million
Number							
1990	36,515	23,231	8,756	2,781	1,102	288	357
1995	41,235	26,001	9,974	3,345	1,234	301	380
1997	42,953	26,928	10,400	3,595	1,324	316	390
1998	43,661	27,317	10,581	3,696	1,354	319	395
1999	44,426	27,696	10,770	3,834	1,398	324	404
2000	45,115	28,062	10,958	3,935	1,424	326	410
2001	45,827	28,474	11,100	4,038	1,466	329	420
Retail Sales (in billions of dollars)							
1990	706.4	205.1	179.5	108.0	91.7	45.1	77.0
1995	893.8	259.6	227.1	136.4	115.8	57.0	97.8
1997	980.0	284.6	249.0	149.7	126.9	62.5	107.4
1998	1,032.4	299.7	262.2	157.7	133.7	65.8	113.2
1999	1,105.3	320.8	280.7	168.9	143.0	70.4	121.4
2000	1,181.1	342.8	300.0	180.5	152.8	75.2	129.8
2001	1,221.7	354.5	310.3	186.8	158.0	77.8	134.4

Source: National Research Business and *Monitor Magazine,* November–December 1991. International Council of Shopping Centers, *Shopping Centers Today,* April 2001.

Through the twentieth century, changing consumer needs drove the development of retail formats. Variety stores that offered wide selections of goods at fixed prices of 5 and 10 cents in the early decades of the century were replaced by large discount operations in the 1950s and 1960s. Neighborhood grocery stores gave way to supermarkets in the 1930s, and warehouse clubs and supercenters now account for increasing proportions of food sales. Specialty stores grew rapidly in number during the 1970s and 1980s, and so-called category killers—stores that offer discount prices and many choices within a narrow category of merchandise—currently dominate the sale of home-improvement products, books, and office supplies.

Southdale, the first fully enclosed shopping mall, opened in Edina, Minnesota, in 1956, and malls with their specialty retailers and department store anchors quickly became popular venues for customers seeking shopping convenience. The late decades of the twentieth century also witnessed the proliferation of many kinds of non-store retailers including television shopping channels, Internet Web sites, and direct mail catalogs.

Retailers add value to products and services by performing four primary functions. First, they create assortments of goods and services; retailers bring together combinations of products or services from numerous sources and offer them in ways that satisfy customer needs. Second, they break bulk: manufacturers produce in large quantities to take advantage of economies of scale; retailers are needed to provide goods in the smaller quantities demanded by consumers. Third, they hold inventory; retailers make products available when and where their customers want them. Fourth, they provide services that facilitate purchasing, for example, credit, product information, extended store hours, and entertainment.

Retailing and the Economy

In the United States, where consumer spending accounts for two-thirds of all economic activity, retail sales in 2000 amounted to more than $3.3 trillion. Retail sales are a major gauge of the nation's economic viability, thus accurate data on the retail industry are needed. To collect this information, the U.S. Census Bureau, relying on the NAICS retail classification system, conducts a number of surveys.

The Monthly Retail Trade Survey has provided data on the value of retail sales each month since 1951. The Annual Retail Trade Survey, which has also been conducted since 1951, monitors the value of retail sales, inventories, and accounts receivable balances. Every five years since 1972, the Census of Retail Trade has been conducted during years ending in 2 and 7. For all retail establishments, the Census Bureau collects data about kind of business, geographic location, organizational status, and number of employees. In 1999 the Census Bureau also began gathering information each quarter related to e-commerce. Although electronic sales accounted for less than 1 percent of total retail sales during the first years of data collection, the e-commerce information permits ongoing assessment of the growth of this retail sector.

Forms of Ownership

Independent, single-store establishments in 1997 accounted for about 60 percent of the more than 1.1 million retail operations in the United States and for approximately $932 billion of the nation's retail sales. Often referred to as "mom and pop" stores, these retailers are frequently owner-managed. They enjoy the advantages of close contact with their customers and flexible operations. However, they lack the economies of scale and management expertise associated with larger retail establishments. To compensate for these shortcomings, independent retailers may join retail-sponsored cooperatives, which operate wholesale buying and distribution systems, or wholesale-sponsored voluntary cooperative groups, which offer buying, distribution, and management assistance in accounting, store layout, employee training, and other areas.

Retail chains operate multiple establishments and employ centralized merchandising and management. Larger chains, which may operate more than 1,000 stores, are corporate-owned and rely upon economies of scale and efficient distribution systems to offer low prices to their customers. Many chains have consolidated. As a result, in 1997, the 50 largest firms accounted for more than 25 percent of retail sales in the United States. Concentration, however, varies by kind of merchandise. In 1997 the four largest furniture stores accounted for only 6.5 percent of sales of furniture and home furnishings; the four largest pharmacies controlled 46.6 percent of pharmacy sales; but the four largest mass merchandisers were responsible for 87.9 percent of sales in that category.

Franchising allows many would-be entrepreneurs the opportunity to own their businesses, while at the same time receiving the benefits of membership in a larger operation. Franchises, which account for more than 30 percent of retail sales in the United States, are based on a formal contract between the franchisee and franchisor. Franchisees pay an initial franchise fee and royalties on sales in exchange for the rights to use the franchisor's logo and operating plan at a specified location. Franchisors monitor their franchisees to assure the quality of products and services, and they assist their franchisees with store location, product/service development, employee training, accounting, and advertising. Violations of the contractual agreement by either franchisor or franchisee may lead to termination of the franchise.

Global Retailing

Thomas Lipton extended his retail operations from England to the United States during the 1890s; a number of retailers of luxury goods, including Burberry and Liberty, established stores outside their home countries in the late nineteenth and early twentieth centuries; and the United States–based F. W. Woolworth Company entered Canada in 1897, England in 1909, and Germany in 1926. During the last decades of the twentieth century, the development of sophisticated communication and transportation systems, saturation of domestic markets, and relaxation of trade barriers greatly accelerated the pace of retail globalization.

International retailing is expensive and risky. Retailers that have succeeded in global

Store display in an F. W. Woolworth's window in Washington, D.C., circa 1920.

ventures have had strong domestic operations and one or more of the following competitive advantages: low cost structure, efficient distribution systems, strong private brands, and a fashion or luxury reputation. They have also been willing to adapt merchandise assortments and store operations to the culture and customs of the host nation. In addition, they have had a long-term commitment to the international market and have been willing to accept low or no profits as they pursued their global efforts.

Leading retailers with operations outside their home country include Wal-Mart (United States), METRO AG (Germany), Carrefour (France), Ahold (Netherlands), Tengelmann (Germany), Tesco (Great Britain), the Aeon Group (Japan), IKEA (Sweden), and Zara (Spain). Global retailers are most interested in markets that have large populations, high per capita spending, or a combination of both. Consequently, Mexico, Latin America, Europe, China, Japan, and the United States are the most frequent targets of retail international expansion efforts. Common methods of entering foreign markets are direct investment, joint venture, strategic alliance, and franchising.

Wholesalers: Who They Are and What They Do

Wholesaling is the sale (as well as the set of activities directly associated with the sale) of goods and services to businesses or organizations for the purposes of: (1) resale, (2) use in producing other goods or services, or (3) operating an organization. The United States Bureau of the Census recognizes three major categories of wholesalers. Merchant wholesalers are independent firms that take title to (own) the products they distribute. Agent wholesaling intermediaries are independent firms that assist in the sale or purchase of products but do not take title to (do not own) the products being distributed. Manufacturer's sales facilities are wholesaling operations owned by manufacturers but physically separated from the parent plants.

Merchant wholesalers are the largest segment of the wholesale trade. Full-service wholesalers provide such services as warehousing, transporting, dividing large quantities, extending credit to customers, reducing producers' risk by taking title to goods, and acting as their customers' purchasing agents. They also offer smaller clients assistance with inventory control and financial management; they inform customers about new products; and they offer suppliers intelligence about changing market needs. Truck jobbers and drop shippers are two other kinds of merchant wholesalers. Truck jobbers deal in limited lines of perishable or time-sensitive goods like snack foods or

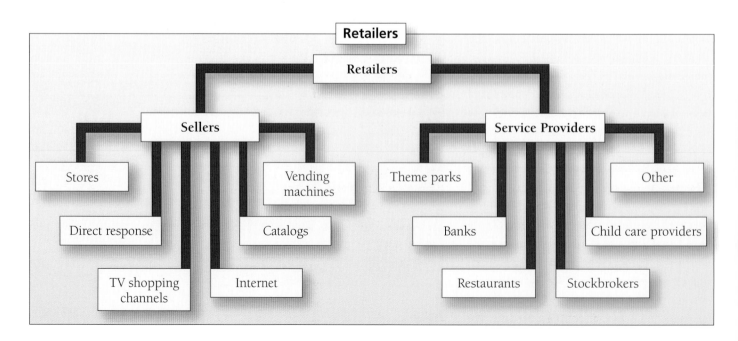

The Internet is an increasingly important venue for retailers to reach their customers.

magazines. They deliver and often shelve the products at retail stores. Drop shippers take title to goods but do not take physical possession of them. Instead, they arrange for products to be delivered directly from producer to customer. They operate in industries like coal and lumber, where products are sold in large quantities and have high freight cost in relation to unit value.

Agent wholesaling intermediaries generally work on commission and perform services related to the buying and selling of products. Manufacturers' agents represent manufacturers of complementary but noncompeting products in assigned geographic areas. They are most likely to be used by small firms that cannot afford their own sales forces, by businesses that add new products not related to existing lines, and by manufacturers that expand into new market areas that are too small to justify sales force expansion. Brokers are another kind of agent wholesaler. They bring buyers and sellers together and provide information, for example, price and product availability. Brokers may work for either the buyer or seller and are commonly found in the food, real estate, and securities industries. Other agent wholesalers include selling agents, who market a seller's entire output; auction companies that sell and provide the facilities for product display; and

import–export agents who assist buyers and sellers from different nations.

Manufacturers' sales facilities are of two kinds—branches and offices. Manufacturers' sales branches carry inventory of the products being sold; manufacturers' sales offices do not.

Wholesaling and the Economy

In 1997 total wholesale sales in the United States amounted to more than $4 trillion. This figure is considerably higher than the $2.4 trillion of retail sales recorded for that year because it includes business goods sold to nonretailers as well as consumer goods that may be handled by several wholesale levels, with sales at each level counted toward total wholesale trade activity. In 1997 more than 453,000 wholesalers operated in the United States; this number had declined from the total of 470,000 in 1992.

The Monthly Wholesale Survey, which tracks sales of merchant wholesalers only, has been conducted each month since 1946. It provides information on the dollar value of wholesale sales and on end-of-the-month inventories. The Annual Wholesale Trade Survey, which also monitors only merchant wholesalers, has been conducted each year since 1978. It gathers data on annual wholesale sales, end-of-year inventories, purchases, and gross margins. The Census of

Merchant Wholesalers: 1990 to 2000

(sales in billions of dollars)

Kind of business	1990	1994	1995	1996	1997	1998	1999	2000
Motor vehicles, parts, and supplies	173.8	188.7	189.0	192.4	195.3	202.6	227.9	199.6
Furniture and home furnishings	33.8	36.9	41.1	43.3	46.7	48.4	50.1	46.5
Lumber and construction materials	63.	79.8	80.0	86.0	90.8	94.4	106.9	71.2
Professional and commercial equipment	114.3	173.0	207.2	229.4	247.5	265.3	281.6	282.7
Metals and minerals, except petroleum	77.7	89.3	95.3	94.2	100.6	97.1	94.3	102.6
Electrical goods	116.4	163.5	193.3	194.7	205.7	210.6	233.0	238.0
Hardware, plumbing and heating equipment	52.6	63.4	67.2	69.9	74.2	78.2	82.1	66.2
Machinery, equipment, and supplies	157.0	176.4	193.5	207.3	225.6	244.1	247.4	253.6
Miscellaneous durable goods	91.4	128.0	143.6	140.9	148.6	140.9	157.0	174.6
Total, durable goods	880.7	1,099.0	1,210.3	1,258.0	1,335.0	1,381.8	1,480.3	1,435.0
Paper and paper products	51.5	66.3	79.5	79.2	83.6	89.6	97.6	80.1
Drugs, proprietaries, and sundries	51.6	76.6	83.9	93.9	107.4	124.4	146.2	166.5
Apparel, piece goods, and notions	64.8	72.6	70.7	75.3	86.3	86.0	92.9	88.6
Groceries and related products	272.4	293.5	312.6	319.2	332.0	346.2	362.9	383.3
Farm-product raw materials	107.6	99.1	119.7	136.8	124.6	107.7	100.1	106.4
Chemicals and allied products	35.7	43.4	50.4	53.3	56.0	55.1	52.9	59.8
Petroleum and petroleum products	148.5	130.5	131.4	148.0	144.4	120.5	144.5	186.6
Beer, wine, and distilled beverages	49.3	52.0	52.6	55.8	58.2	61.6	66.8	71.2
Miscellaneous nondurable goods	130.8	143.0	159.7	171.4	173.4	181.2	196.2	174.2
Total, nondurable goods	912.3	976.9	1,060.6	1,133.0	1,165.8	1,172.3	1,260.2	1,316.7
Total, merchant wholesalers	1,792.9	2,075.9	2,271.0	2,391.0	2,500.9	2,554.1	2,740.5	2,751.8

Source: U.S. Bureau of the Census, *Current Business Reports, Annual Benchmark Report for Wholesale Trade, January 1990–February 2002.*

Wholesale Trade has taken place in each year ending in a 2 or 7 since 1972. The Census Bureau tracks all kinds of wholesalers and includes data on kind of business, geographic location, value of sales sold by commission, and commission rates.

Retail and Wholesale Costs

The participation of retailers and wholesalers in distribution channels raises the costs of goods for consumers. The operating expense of retailers is estimated at approximately 28 percent of retail sales, while the operating expense of wholesalers is about 8 percent of retail sales. These costs are considerable, but the important functions these intermediaries perform in making goods and services readily available to the consumer justify the expenses.

Electronic commerce offers the possibility of increasing the efficiency of some functions now performed by retailers and wholesalers.

E-commerce will not eliminate retail and wholesale marketing intermediaries, at least not for the foreseeable future, but it has and will continue to change the nature of the game for both retailers and wholesalers.

Further Reading

Alexander, Nicholas. *International Retailing.* Oxford: Blackwell, 1997.

Bradach, Jeffrey. *Franchise Organizations.* Boston: Harvard Business School Publishing, 1998.

Plunkett-Powell, Karen. *Remembering Woolworth: A Nostalgic History of the World's Most Famous Five and Dime.* New York: St. Martin's Press, 2001.

Roush, Chris. *Inside Home Depot: How One Company Revolutionized an Industry through Relentless Pursuit of Growth.* New York: McGraw-Hill, 1999.

Underhill, Paco. *Why We Buy: The Science of Shopping.* New York: Simon & Schuster, 2000.

Wendt, Lloyd, and Herman Kogan. *Give the Lady What She Wants! The Story of Marshall Field and Company.* Chicago: Rand McNally, 1952.

—*Marilyn Lavin*

Reverse Engineering

When a complicated product is developed to perform a certain task—for example, when an automobile is developed that can accelerate very quickly or a drug is developed to stop a migraine headache—the product is said to be engineered to do that task. Reverse engineering is the opposite. When a product is reverse engineered, a person looks at the tasks a finished product can do and then essentially takes the product apart to see how it performs its task. Just about anything can be, and is, reverse engineered, from cosmetics and machinery to drugs and computer software. Genetic scientists even talk about reverse engineering genes to determine their exact chemical makeup. Although reverse engineering has legitimate uses, it can be used to engage in illegal practices, for example, patent infringement and cracking security systems.

Reverse engineering occupies a gray area in the world of business. Obviously, the person who engineered a particular product has no need to reverse engineer it as she already knows how it works. Reverse engineering is done by someone else—a competitor or some other outsider—who wants to know more about how a particular product works. Reverse engineering is quite common; companies specializing in reverse engineering of high-technology goods are regularly engaged by businesses. Generally, however, businesses do not readily reveal that they reverse engineer their competitors' products.

When researchers want to reverse engineer something, they examine what it does.

See also:
Copyright; Intellectual Property; Patent; Research and Development; Technology.

Reverse engineering involves taking a commercial product apart and analyzing the parts to discover how it was made.

Then they work backward to determine how the object or process does what it does. They often take the item apart, try to analyze all its components, and then try to determine how they all work together. For example, companies that reverse engineer computer chips buy a chip commercially. They then remove metal connectors, as well as special laminates that chip manufacturers put on their chips to hamper such reverse engineering, until the inner workings of the chip are exposed. Then, they examine those inner workings with optical and electron microscopes and X-ray machines, essentially photographing the intricate miniature circuitry that lies on the chip. A knowledgeable chip manufacturer can examine those images to determine if a competitor is using a revolutionary new design or is pilfering a patented design from the patent holder. Performance tests on the chips can give even more insight into their workings.

Reverse engineering has many uses that are not at all controversial. For example, if a machine part that is no longer manufactured breaks, a company will often reverse engineer the part rather than scrap the entire machine. Or a company might have a database that works very well and is easy to use, but the underlying computer language is so old that the company cannot make the database accessible on the Internet. This process is a form of reverse engineering that is sometimes known as reengineering. Reengineering involves analyzing old software, usually called legacy software, and deciding what about the system worked well and what did not. The useful parts of the legacy software are saved (or mined) and new software is written around those aspects. For example, the company might hire programmers to reengineer the database using a newer computer language so that the database does everything it used to do but now can be accessed via the Web. Reengineering can be a vital strategy for many businesses because so much legacy software exists and because it can be prohibitively expensive to redesign entirely new systems or purchase them outright from outside sources.

Software makers often reverse engineer software made by other companies by figuring out the underlying source code of the program. Often makers of software will reverse engineer popular programs that will have to interface with the software they are developing to make sure the new software will work well with programs customers are likely to have on their computers. Likewise, makers of video games will reverse engineer the software found in video-game players to ensure that their games run smoothly.

Controversial Uses of Reverse Engineering

Other uses of reverse engineering are less savory. The Chinese military, for example, is believed to rely heavily on the reverse engineering of American military technology to improve its own weaponry. The military reportedly purchases old American matériel that comes to market and observes up-to-date matériel in action when the United States engages in military activity.

In the private sector, reverse engineering can give rise to products made by different companies that are remarkably similar, as each company disassembles and mimics its competitors' products. If reverse engineering is done ethically, each company will have devised its own methods of developing products that do roughly the same thing. Even so, the result is many very similar products. Heavy reliance on reverse engineering is not a road map for innovation.

Reverse engineering is also almost a necessary ingredient for piracy, or the outright copying of products. Piracy is widespread in less developed nations, where copyright laws are weak, enforcement is lax, and piracy is often viewed as a way to make products more affordable. In India, for example, companies routinely reverse engineer pharmaceuticals and produce their own, cheaper versions of the drugs. Software piracy is also a serious problem in many less developed nations.

In addition, reverse engineering can pose a significant threat to information security. Reverse engineering an encryption

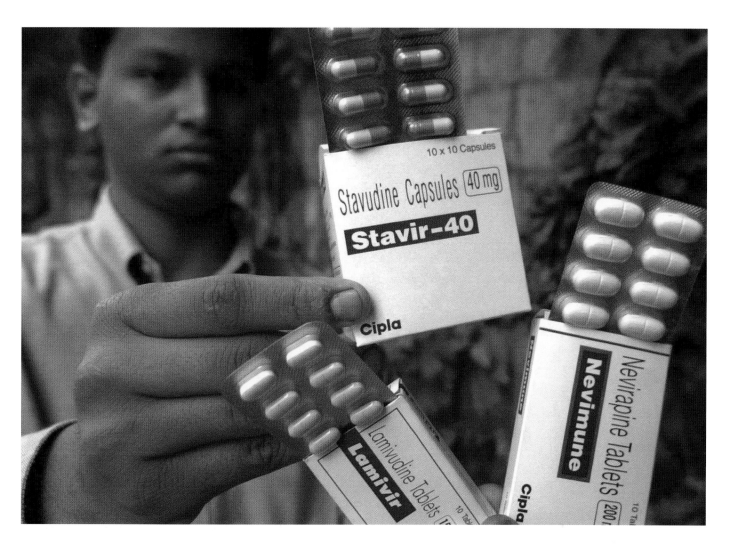

program, for example, can give hackers valuable insight into a program's weaknesses. By determining how a program scrambles a digital communication, hackers can often find a way to unscramble the communication. Reverse engineering has always had a somewhat shady reputation, but the reverse engineering of software, especially of encryption programs, has made the practice especially controversial. Even in the United States, which has strong copyright laws, reverse engineering itself is not illegal—what is illegal is the copying and selling of software source code or patented formulas and methodologies discovered by reverse engineering.

The problems of security and piracy faced by the software industry have led to calls to restrict the reverse engineering of software. As a practical matter, such restrictions would be very difficult to enforce, and, as the practice does have legitimate uses, restrictions on reverse engineering could hamper ordinary business activities. At the moment, reverse engineering will likely remain legal, a tool that can be used for both good and ill.

Further Reading

Aiken, Peter. *Data Reverse Engineering: Slaying the Legacy Dragon.* New York: McGraw-Hill, 1996.
Cringely, Robert X. *Accidental Empires: How the Boys of Silicon Valley Make Their Millions, Battle Foreign Competition, and Still Can't Get a Date.* Rev. and expanded ed. New York: HarperBusiness, 1996.
Lim, Wayne C. *Managing Software Reuse: A Comprehensive Guide to Strategically Reengineering the Organization for Reusable Components.* Upper Saddle River, N.J.: Prentice Hall, 1998.
Miller, Howard W. *Reengineering Legacy Software Systems.* Boston: Digital Press, 1998.
Wills, Linda, and Philip Newcomb, eds. *Reverse Engineering.* Boston: Kluwer Academic Publishers, 1996.

—*Mary Sisson*

A marketing executive at the Indian firm Cipla Ltd. poses with an anti-AIDS drug in the company's export boardroom in 2001. Indian pharmaceutical companies making cheap, generic anti-AIDS drugs are viewing a landmark case in South Africa as a lucrative opening for their products in the developing world.

See also:
Commodities;
Entrepreneurship;
Insurance Industry.

Risk Management

Risk refers to the possibility of loss or injury, especially in situations marked by uncertainty. People put themselves at risk by driving on icy roads, by investing in the stock market, and by petting a strange dog; everything might turn out fine, but each action also might lead to trouble, minor or serious. The variation in possible outcomes creates the sense of risk.

In day-to-day operations, businesses always take some degree of risk: the new supplier might be unreliable, the new product line might not appeal to customers, or the chief financial officer might embezzle money. The potential loss lies in the future in each case, and the future is uncertain. Risk management refers to business practices designed to reduce the possibilities of loss that arise from uncertain knowledge about the future.

Aspects of Risk Management

Risk management involves three steps: identifying sources of potential losses, evaluating potential losses, and selecting means for responding to loss exposures. After these steps are completed, businesses and individuals can implement and administer a risk management program.

Identifying Sources of Potential Losses. People who study risk describe potential losses by reference to different kinds of sources: perils, hazards, and exposures. A peril is an immediate cause of a loss. Common perils include fire, hail, tornadoes, earthquakes, and hurricanes.

A hazard is a more general condition that lies behind the occurrence of a loss, increasing its probability of occurrence, its severity, or both. Some hazards are physical conditions in the environment that increase the risk of loss. Examples might include a poorly lit stairwell in an apartment building or old, frayed wiring in a warehouse. Other hazards are moral: conditions in which somebody or some organization might benefit from a loss and might therefore have reason to feel ambivalent about the risk in question. If an insurance policy guarantees reimbursement for the cost of a new computer when an old one is stolen, for example, the insured owner of an old computer may be less than diligent about preventing its theft. The moral hazard in such a case need not involve outright dishonesty. It might be a matter of inattention or carelessness augmented by the prospect of benefiting from loss.

Exposure in a risk situation is the kind of loss faced by the person or company at risk. A property loss exposure is associated with real property (a beachfront hotel might be leveled by a hurricane, for example) and personal property (an automobile might get dented). A liability exposure involves the

Sources of Risks

Type	Definition	Examples
Peril	• An immediate cause of loss	• Fire • Tornadoes • Earthquakes • Terrorism
Hazard	• Physical conditions in the environment that increase risk of loss • Moral conditions in which someone might benefit from a loss	• Physical: poorly lit stairway • Moral: insurance policy guaranteeing replacement of stolen property
Exposure	• Type of loss faced by person or company at risk	• Property loss: personal or real property • Liability: lawsuits

possibility that a person or business might face lawsuits (a restaurant might be sued by a customer alleging food poisoning, for example) and therefore incur an obligation to pay money damages.

Managing risk uses various methods to identify potential losses. One approach is the physical inspection of a business or home to identify potential perils, hazards, and exposures. Inspectors from an insurance company might advise owners of a nursing home, for example, that they face a risk of liability arising from inadequate supervision of aides. Some potential losses can be anticipated by reviews that identify losses that have occurred in the past. An analysis of a firm's financial statements might provide clues to the present loss exposures of the firm. Businesses may also use risk questionnaires and interviews with employees to learn about areas of potential exposure. By identifying problems, businesses decrease their chance of ignoring exposures that could lead to catastrophic losses.

Evaluating Potential Losses. The second step in the risk management process is to evaluate potential losses, estimating their probable frequency and severity. Loss frequency is the probable number of losses that may occur during a given period—for example, the number of accidents a business's fleet of delivery trucks is likely to be involved with in the next year. Loss severity is the potential size of the losses. From frequency and severity estimates, potential loss exposures can be ranked. Ranking enables an individual or business to decide which loss exposures deserve the most attention.

Responding to Loss Exposures. The third step in risk management is to consider various responses to loss exposures. Businesses rely on two main approaches: risk control and risk financing.

Risk control involves techniques that reduce the frequency and severity of losses, including avoidance of certain hazards and implementation of safety programs. Just as an individual can avoid the risk of being

Underwriters at Lloyd's of London in England, undated photo.

killed in a bungee cord accident by finding another recreational activity, a business can avoid some liability exposures by declining to offer certain products or services. Insurance companies prohibited by state law from linking their prices (insurance premiums) to varying degrees of risk, for example, may respond by withdrawing from that sector of the insurance market.

Living with Risk

Avoiding all risks is impossible; it is also undesirable. One could avoid the peril of

Steps in Dealing with Risk

Identify sources of potential losses

⬇

Evaluate potential for exposure

⬇

Respond to loss exposures
(such as risk control and risk financing)

automobile crashes by refusing ever to ride in an automobile, but the alternatives—riding a horse, walking, staying home—would strike many people as unsatisfactory and would, in any case, introduce new forms of risk. Risk is associated, moreover, with positive outcomes as well as losses. Some economists contend that profitable economic activity is linked with risks taken in a climate of uncertainty. For

individuals and businesses, therefore, acting to control the frequency, severity, or unpredictability of losses that cannot be avoided is the preferred course. The frequency of fires might be reduced by prohibiting smoking in areas with flammables present, for example; losses from fires might also be reduced by the installation of sprinkler systems.

To handle risks that cannot be avoided or adequately controlled, individuals and businesses often turn to some form of risk financing. One kind of risk financing is risk retention. An individual practices risk retention when he or she knows of a certain risk and decides nonetheless to keep at least part of it. For example, a driver may decide to retain the risk of a fender bender (in part) by purchasing a car insurance policy with a $500 deductible (driver agrees to pay for all damage to the car

A crystal and glass gift shop in Olympia, Washington, after an earthquake in 2001.

under $500). He retains $500 worth of risk, and in return his insurance premiums are reduced. Alternatively, the driver could choose to adopt a funded risk-retention program by setting money aside to pay for damage to his car in case of an accident.

Another kind of risk financing is transfer—a shifting over of risk to somebody else by means of a legal agreement. Transfer may be achieved through contracts, hedging, incorporation of a business, or the purchase of insurance. Transfer of risk by contract occurs, for example, when a purchaser of an automobile also purchases an extended warranty. The risk of loss from defects in the automobile is then shifted to the issuer of the warranty. Hedging is a means for transferring the risk of unfavorable price increases by buying and selling contracts on an organized exchange like the Chicago Board of Trade or New York Stock Exchange. For example, Southwest Airlines reduces the risk of spikes in aviation fuel prices by buying contracts for the delivery of set amounts of aviation fuel at a fixed price at a known date in the future. Some business owners shift risk by incorporation. Laws governing incorporation generally prevent business creditors from taking personal assets belonging to owners, even when the owner's business owes a debt.

For many individuals and businesses, insurance is the most feasible method for transferring risk. It often provides a relatively inexpensive means to address potential losses. In return for premium payments, the insurer agrees to pay for certain losses in the event of specified contingencies, for example, illness or a failed shipment of goods. The insuring company can offer such protection because it pools risks from a large group of individuals or businesses—betting, in effect, that only a small percentage of them will make valid claims in a given year.

The purchaser of insurance must avoid buying either too little or too much protection. Insufficient coverage may leave the purchaser vulnerable to huge financial losses. Buying too much insurance, however, shifts

risk that might better be retained. Risk is present even in efforts to reduce risk.

Risk is uncertainty about the occurrence of a loss. Minimizing the negative aspects of not knowing the future is the essence of risk management. Risk management entails identifying potential losses, evaluating them, selecting appropriate means for responding to loss exposures, and implementing a risk management program. Insurance is the most common technique used for managing risk.

A company that relies on a fleet of trucks might need to evaluate its loss frequency—the probable number of lost or damaged trucks during a given time.

Further Reading

Bernstein, P. L. *Against the Gods: The Remarkable Story of Risk.* New York: John Wiley & Sons, 1996.

Harrington, S., and G. Niehaus. *Risk Management and Insurance.* Boston: Irwin/McGraw-Hill, 1999.

Vaughan, E. *Risk Management.* New York: John Wiley & Sons, 1997.

Williams, C., Peter Young, and Michael Smith. *Risk Management and Insurance.* 8th ed. New York: McGraw-Hill, 1998.

—*Carl Pacini*

See also:
Monopoly; Price Fixing;
Sherman Antitrust Act;
Standard Oil; Texaco.

Rockefeller, John D.

1839–1937
Oil magnate

John D. Rockefeller began earning money at the age of 12 and never looked back. During his life, he became one of the wealthiest men in America, as well as one of the most reviled. Rockefeller was known for ruthless business tactics, yet during his life he gave away almost all of his fortune to charities. He created a powerful American dynasty whose influence long outlived him.

Early Years

John D. Rockefeller was born in Tioga County, New York, on July 8, 1839. His father, William Avery Rockefeller, traveled the country selling cancer "cures" and patent medicines. His mother, Eliza Davison Rockefeller, was a religious disciplinarian who taught John the virtues of hard work and savings. John's career as an entrepreneur started early. When he was 12 he earned $50 from doing chores for neighbors, then lent the money to a local farmer at 7 percent interest.

In 1853 the Rockefeller family moved to Cleveland, Ohio, where John attended high school. He excelled at math and public

speaking but was otherwise an average student. In 1855 he dropped out of high school to spend 10 weeks at Folsom Commercial College, learning bookkeeping and other business skills. In September 1855 Rockefeller got a job as an assistant bookkeeper with Hewitt & Tuttle, a small firm of commission merchants and produce shippers. He impressed his employers with his seriousness, dedication, and honesty and was soon engaged in making complicated transportation arrangements that involved moving freight by boat and railroad.

In 1859 Rockefeller went into the commission business with another young broker, Maurice B. Clark. On August 27 of that same year, Edwin Drake struck oil near Titusville, Pennsylvania. The discovery that oil could be removed from the ground by drilling launched the petroleum industry and changed Rockefeller's life.

Rockefeller realized that the future of the agricultural shipping business in Cleveland was limited. He believed that the future lay in the shipment of raw industrial materials—especially petroleum. In 1863 Rockefeller joined with oil refiner Samuel Andrews, Maurice Clark, and Clark's two brothers to form the oil refining firm of Andrews, Clark & Company. Rockefeller wanted to borrow money to expand the refining business, but the Clarks resisted. So, in February of 1865, Rockefeller bought

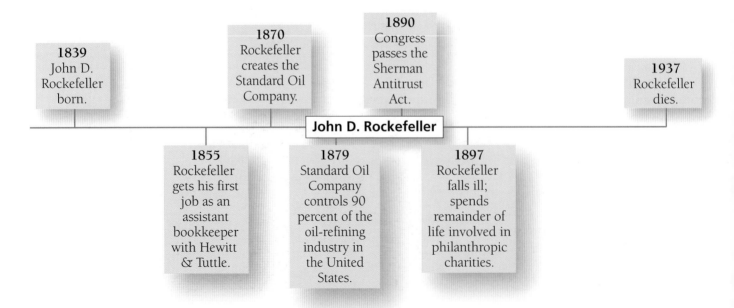

1839
John D.
Rockefeller
born.

1855
Rockefeller
gets his first
job as an
assistant
bookkeeper
with Hewitt
& Tuttle.

1870
Rockefeller
creates the
Standard Oil
Company.

1879
Standard Oil
Company
controls 90
percent of the
oil-refining
industry in
the United
States.

1890
Congress
passes the
Sherman
Antitrust
Act.

John D. Rockefeller

1897
Rockefeller
falls ill;
spends
remainder of
life involved in
philanthropic
charities.

1937
Rockefeller
dies.

out the Clarks for $72,500 and gained complete control of the business.

Rockefeller immediately began borrowing heavily and reinvesting all his profits into the business. In 1867 he joined another self-made businessman, Henry M. Flagler, and formed Rockefeller, Andrews & Flagler. By 1868 this company was the largest oil refiner in the world.

The Standard Oil Company

At that time the oil business was chaotic. Because setting up oil drilling and oil refining plants cost very little, the market was glutted with both crude oil and refined products, and prices fluctuated wildly. Rockefeller decided that the solution was to have only one huge oil organization that controlled everything—from drilling to refining and shipping—and that the huge organization should be his. On January 10, 1870, John Rockefeller created the Standard Oil Company of Ohio with his brother William Rockefeller, Henry Flagler, Samuel Andrews, Stephen Harkness, and O. B. Jennings (William Rockefeller's brother-in-law).

Rockefeller, driven and determined, was known for his iron will and his emphasis on controlling costs and improving efficiency at every level. He believed that the best way to accomplish his goal was to implement what is now called vertical integration: own and control every aspect of the business from raw product to the shipping and sale of the finished goods.

In December 1871 Rockefeller began, in great secrecy, to consolidate the oil industry. He started by buying all the refineries in Cleveland. His technique was always the same. The owners of each refinery were told that most of the other refineries had already agreed. They would be given Standard Oil stock in exchange for their business and made partners in Standard Oil. By spring 1872 Rockefeller had bought or merged with almost all the refineries in Cleveland. The sheer size of the business gave Rockefeller tremendous leverage with the railroads. He was able to negotiate big rebates from the railroads, which gave Rockfeller's refineries an advantage over other refiners.

John D. Rockefeller in an undated photo.

Rockefeller then began building oil pipelines and terminal facilities, purchasing competing refineries in other cities, and expanding markets in the United States and abroad. By 1879 the Standard Oil Company controlled about 90 percent of the oil refining industry in the United States and about 40 percent of the world export market—and Rockefeller, just 40 years old, controlled Standard. In 1881 Rockefeller and his associates placed the stock of Standard of Ohio and its affiliates in other states under the control of a board of nine trustees, with Rockefeller at the head. This was the first major U.S. trust and set a pattern for other monopolies.

The aggressive competitive practices of Standard Oil and the growing public hostility to monopolies, of which Standard was the best known, led to the passage by the U.S. Congress of the Sherman Antitrust Act (1890). In response, Rockefeller dissolved the trust and transferred its properties to companies in other states. In 1911 the U.S. Supreme Court found the major component of the reorganized trust, Standard Oil Company, in violation of the Sherman Antitrust Act and ordered it dismantled.

A Second Career

During 1891 and 1892 Rockefeller lost all of his hair, including his eyebrows, and suffered from ill health, possibly brought on by overwork. He stopped going into the office every day and retired in 1897 at the age of 58.

Rockefeller decided to spend his time giving away money instead of earning it. Together with his son, John D., Jr., Rockefeller created major philanthropic institutions, including the University of Chicago (which received $75 million); the Rockefeller Institute for Medical Research (now Rockefeller University); the Rockefeller Foundation; and the General Education Board in 1903 (later the Rockefeller Foundation), to which Rockefeller gave $50 million to establish high schools throughout the South and to raise teaching salaries in the region.

During his lifetime, Rockefeller gave away more than $500 million. By 1955 the foundations Rockefeller had established had given away more than $2.5 billion.

Rockefeller had a great impact on the way that goods and services are manufactured and distributed. Although the trust system was found to be illegal and unscrupulous, it did result in an increased emphasis on efficiency in production and distribution and created the modern oil industry. After retiring, Rockefeller became one of the greatest philanthropists America has ever known. His legacy remains a contradictory one of both unsavory business practices and great philanthropy and good works.

The Rockefeller Family

John D. Rockefeller's influence did not end with his death. His family remained one of the most influential in America; two members of that family in particular—Nelson Rockefeller and John D. Rockefeller, Jr.—would prove very influential.

JOHN D. ROCKEFELLER, JR. (1874–1960)
Born on January 29, 1874, John D., Jr., was the youngest of four children and the only boy. John Jr. readily absorbed the strict discipline and frugal lifestyle inculcated by his parents. "My mother and father raised but one question: Is it right, is it duty?" he would recall years later. While attending Brown University, he became interested in the new theories of labor and social reform that were becoming popular.

In 1896 John Jr. entered the Standard Oil business, but by 1910 he had become disenchanted with the business and the controversies that had erupted around it and decided to cut all ties with the Standard Oil trust and devote himself to philanthropy.

John Jr. initiated and pushed forward many Rockefeller philanthropic endeavors, including the creation of the Rockefeller Institute for Medical Research (now Rockefeller University), the General Education Board, the restoration of Colonial Williamsburg, and the construction of Rockefeller Center.

In 1946 he gave $8 million for the creation of the United Nations building in New York. During John Jr.'s lifetime, his charitable gifts are estimated to have totaled $537 million. He died in Tucson, Arizona, in 1960, at the age of 86.

NELSON ALDRICH ROCKEFELLER (1908–1979)
Nelson Rockefeller was born on July 8, 1908. After graduating from Dartmouth College in 1930 with a degree in economics, Nelson spent the next 10 years working in several of the family businesses. His interest in Latin America led him to take a position in 1940 as coordinator of inter-American affairs at the State Department. He rose to the position of assistant secretary of state for Latin American affairs. He left government service in 1945 to help found a private nonprofit group to help developing nations in Latin America.

He returned to government service and served as undersecretary of the newly created Department of Health, Education, and Welfare from 1953 to 1955. Nelson Rockefeller became governor of New York in 1958 and was reelected governor in 1962, 1966, and 1970. In 1973 Rockefeller lost a fourth bid for the Republican presidential nomination, but the following year he was chosen as the 41st vice president of the United States by Gerald Ford (Ford, the 40th vice president, had become president following the resignation of Richard Nixon).

Rockefeller was a supporter of the liberal wing of the Republican Party. His liberal ideas and proposals grew increasingly unpopular in the conservative Republican Party. His political career ended with the end of the Ford presidency. Nelson Rockefeller died on January 26, 1979.

Further Readings
Chernow, Ron. *Titan: The Life of John D. Rockefeller.* New York: Vantage Books. 1999.
Rockefeller, John D., Jr. *Dear Father/Dear Son: Correspondence of John D. Rockefeller and John D. Rockefeller, Jr.* Edited by Joseph W. Ernst. New York: Fordham University Press, 1994.
Smith, George David, and Frederick Dalzell. *Wisdom from the Robber Barons: Enduring Business Lessons from Rockefeller, Morgan, and the First Industrialists.* Cambridge, Mass.: Perseus Publishing, 2000.

—Lisa Magloff

Royal Bank of Canada

Royal Bank of Canada is Canada's largest financial institution both in terms of assets (what the company owns) and as measured by market capitalization (the market value of its issued share capital). It is one of North America's leading diversified financial services companies; its services include personal and commercial banking, wealth management, insurance, corporate and investment banking, and transaction processing services on a global basis. The company's head office is in Montreal, Quebec, though much of its business is centered in Toronto, Canada's premier financial city. The company uses the initials RBC as a prefix for its businesses and operating subsidiaries, which operate under the master brand name of RBC Financial Group. RBC employs more than 60,000 people and has operations in approximately 30 countries around the world.

RBC's history closely parallels the economic and political history of Canada itself. The bank actually predates the 1867 founding of the Canadian Confederation. The institution's origins lie in Halifax, Nova Scotia, where it was formed in 1864 by a small group of businessmen as the Merchants Bank. Initially, the Merchants Bank invested in the Nova Scotian staple industries of fishing and lumber, as well as in the import of goods into what was then a British colony. The Dominion of Canada became a self-governing confederation in 1867, and the Bank Act of 1869 required banks to have a federal charter. The Merchants Bank was chartered as the Merchants Bank of Halifax in 1869. During the following two decades, the bank expanded into the other Canadian maritime provinces of Prince Edward Island and New Brunswick.

A key moment in the bank's development was its securing of a foothold in Montreal in 1887, a time when the city was at the center of Canadian financial activity. This signaled the continentalization of the bank's interests, in the sense that it came to focus more on opening branches across Canada than on its established regional base in the Canadian maritime provinces. As the Canadian West was opened up by the completion of the Canadian Pacific Railway in 1883, the bank established branches in British Columbia, Manitoba, Saskatchewan, and Alberta. Once established as a national operation, the bank changed its name to The Royal Bank of Canada in 1901. To reflect its new national status, the bank moved its headquarters westward to Montreal in 1907.

The bank's growth was often achieved through amalgamations with other banks, a process that led to its emergence as the largest bank in Canada by 1920. RBC's first international expansion was into the Caribbean in the late nineteenth century, founding an agency in Bermuda in 1882. From a base in Havana, Cuba, established in March 1899, the bank rapidly developed interests throughout Latin America in the first three decades of the twentieth century. Over the same period, it began operations in key financial centers, such as New York, London, and Paris.

The Wall Street Crash of October 1929, and the international Depression that followed, placed banks under enormous pressure during the first half of the 1930s. Governments initially responded to the crisis with deflationary policies, and the tight lending practices of the banks were the public face of those policies. Banks became deeply unpopular; the fortunes

See also:
Great Depression; Hudson's Bay Company.

Merchants' Bank of Halifax staff, 1880.

Royal Bank chairman John Cleghorn, right, and Bank of Montreal chairman Matthew Barrett shake hands after a news conference in Toronto in January 1998 to announce a merger deal between the two banks.

of the banking industry were not restored until World War II. During World War II, RBC played a leading role in financing Canada's contribution to the Allied war effort and, along with other Canadian chartered banks, administered numerous government programs on its behalf, including the sale of Victory Bonds and the redemption of ration coupons.

In the prosperous 1950s and 1960s, the bank expanded its range of consumer services to include personal checking accounts, new forms of personal loans, the issuing of credit cards, and automated banking. Following the discovery of vast oil reserves in Alberta in 1947, the bank provided initial funding for the development of the province's oil industry. The second half of the twentieth century saw the bank continue its international expansion.

Like other leading banks, RBC came under strain in the 1980s, an era of high interest rates and a resultant global economic crisis as Third World countries defaulted on their debts. It was also a time when the banking industry was sharply deregulated. These policies heralded rapid changes in the operations of all of Canada's financial institutions as the Canadian market for their products was opened to international competition. In 1990 The Royal Bank of Canada dropped the definite article from its title and became simply Royal Bank of Canada.

Beginning in 1995 with its listing on the New York Stock Exchange (under the stock symbol, RY), RBC has pursued a strategy of vigorous North American expansion through the acquisition of such U.S.–based assets as Prism Financial Corporation (2000), Liberty Life and Liberty Insurance Services (2000), Centura Banks, Incorporated (2001), Dain Rauscher Corporation (2001), Tucker Anthony Sutro (2001), Eagle Bancshares, Incorporated (2002), the Private Banking Operations of Barclays Bank PLC in the Americas (2002), and Admiralty Bancorp, Incorporated (2003).

Further Reading

McDowall, Duncan. *Quick to the Frontier: Canada's Royal Bank*. Toronto: McClelland & Stewart, 1993.

—*Peter C. Grosvenor*

Royal Dutch/Shell

The red-and-yellow Shell symbol is among the most universally recognized corporate logos in the world. It is the emblem of the Royal Dutch/Shell Group of companies, often referred to simply as Shell. In 2002 Shell employed 91,000 people, operated 46,000 gas stations, and owned an interest in 53 petroleum refineries worldwide. Its net income was $10.85 billion. Formed by a unique merger in 1907 between Royal Dutch Petroleum and the English Shell Transport & Trading Company, Royal Dutch/Shell grew to become one of the towering giants in the petroleum industry, an industry whose prominence in the twentieth century is virtually unrivaled.

Origins

The alliance between Royal Dutch and Shell came about through an unlikely pairing of two strong personalities. Marcus Samuel had inherited a small fortune from his father, who had imported from Asia, among other things, seashells, which were used for decoration and jewelry. In the 1890s Marcus Samuel expanded the London business into kerosene, lighting fuel refined from oil. Samuel organized a new system of distributing kerosene in the East by bulk tanker shipments. The tankers were named after seashells, thus the origin of the Shell trademark. In 1898 Samuel combined his growing Far East syndicate of businesses into the Shell Transport & Trading Company. The company soon became locked in fierce competition with Standard Oil, the giant trust created by John D. Rockefeller, who was known for mercilessly undermining and then swallowing competitors.

Samuel and Rockefeller both coveted oil-producing properties in the Dutch East Indies, where the Royal Dutch Petroleum Company had established itself as a successful oil producer. Under the leadership of Henri Wilhelm August Deterding, who had risen to become a managing director of Royal Dutch at the age of 34, Royal Dutch had grown into a substantial integrated oil company, combining oil exploration, production, and refining. Seeing mutual advantages in an alliance to resist the takeover maneuvers and price-cutting tactics of the formidable Standard Oil, Deterding and Samuel resolved to combine their companies.

The two companies reached an unusual agreement. They united their interests, but retained separate identities. All oil lands and refineries were transferred to a newly formed Dutch company, N.V. De Bataafsche Petroleum Maatschappij (the Bavarian Petroleum Company), headquartered in

See also:
Energy Industry;
Organization of Petroleum
Exporting Countries.

A Shell Oil offshore drilling platform is towed toward the Gulf of Mexico through the Corpus Christi Ship Channel in Texas.

The Hague. An English firm, the Anglo-Saxon Petroleum Company, located in London, took over all transportation and storage assets. Both Royal Dutch and Shell became holding companies for these new operating companies. Each of these companies and their subsidiaries was a legal entity, together composing the Royal Dutch/Shell Group. Five managing directors—two from Shell and three from Royal Dutch—oversaw this unique enterprise, but during the next 30 years (until his retirement in 1936), Deterding was the key figure presiding over Royal Dutch/Shell's expanding empire, the only one that could truly rival Standard Oil

and its offspring after Rockefeller's company was broken up in 1911.

Decentralized Expansion

After the merger, Royal Dutch/Shell spread around the world, registering its trademark pecten, or scallop shell, in Europe, the Middle East, Asia, Australia, parts of Africa, and the Americas. The mass production of automobiles in the United States and Europe created soaring demand for gasoline and lucrative new markets for oil firms.

Shell entered the United States in 1912, supplying gasoline to the Pacific Northwest. Subsequently, it stretched down the coast into exploration and production in California and then broadened the hunt for oil into Oklahoma. Shell Oil, the name of the chief U.S. operating subsidiary, became one of the most successful enterprises in the sprawling Royal Dutch/Shell family. After World War II, Shell Oil assumed unparalleled leadership in the new offshore frontier, developing the first semi-submersible drilling vessel in the early 1960s and pioneering advances in exploration geophysics and the enhanced recovery of oil from old fields. During much of the postwar period, Shell Oil accounted for nearly one-third of the Royal Dutch/Shell Group's overall profits.

The increasingly decentralized organization of Royal Dutch/Shell permitted foreign subsidiaries like Shell Oil room to grow and flourish in their distinct cultural and political environments. Top managers supervised and coordinated the company's far-flung operations, but refrained from managing day-to-day operations of the nearly 500 companies owned wholly, jointly, and indirectly by Royal Dutch/Shell. After the Mexican government expropriated oil wells of the Shell subsidiary, El Aquila, in 1938, Shell became one of the first multinational companies to recognize the social and political appeal of employing qualified nationals in positions of authority—to give at least the appearance of local control.

Managing director John Hugo Loudon anticipated growing nationalistic trends and

Royal Dutch/Shell

1898
Marcus Samuel creates the Shell Transport & Trading Company.

1907
A merger results in the Royal Dutch/Shell Group.

1912
Royal Dutch/Shell enters the United States.

1959
John Hugo Loudon leads the company's development of new oil sources.

1973
Oil embargo triples prices for crude oil.

1998
Royal Dutch/Shell embarks on a radical restructuring program, cutting costs and personnel.

A girl passes oil pipes running through her neighborhood in Port Harcourt, Nigeria.

urged the hiring of more citizens of host countries in executive positions. As head of the group's committee of managing directors from 1959 to 1965, Loudon steered the company back to international prominence. Under his leadership, it developed important new sources of oil in Oman and Nigeria, expanded production from traditional suppliers like Venezuela and Iraq, and outstripped all other oil companies in the production of chemicals.

Despite the strong push in oil exploration during the 1950s and 1960s, Royal Dutch/Shell was still a "crude short" operation—its own crude oil supplies were not enough to meet the demands of its vast transportation, refining, and marketing system. Shell had to purchase much more crude oil than the other major oil companies, which possessed greater shares of Middle East oil. This was not a significant problem for Royal Dutch/Shell during the so-called buyer's market of the 1960s, when oil prices remained in the $2 to $3 per barrel range. The Organization of Petroleum Exporting Countries (OPEC) oil embargo of 1973, however, put Shell in a difficult position: as crude prices tripled, governments of producing countries took control of local oil industries.

Reinvention

The OPEC oil embargo ushered in a 30-year period of price volatility and industry instability. Royal Dutch/Shell survived the 1970s by diversifying into other energy businesses, for example, coal and nuclear power. A more successful strategy involved developing new sources of oil and gas offshore, especially in the North Sea, deepwater Gulf of Mexico, and eventually West Africa. The depression in oil prices during the 1980s and 1990s played to Royal Dutch/Shell's downstream strengths, allowing it to manage for the long term, rather than focus on squeezing out short-term profits. Nevertheless, as the century closed, the company faced daunting challenges, including widespread environmental opposition in Europe to its plan to sink Brent Spar, an oil storage installation in the North Sea. Royal Dutch/Shell was also the target of fierce criticism on human rights issues, stemming from the Nigerian government's execution of Ken Saro-Wiwa, a prominent Nigerian author who protested Shell's environmental record in his country.

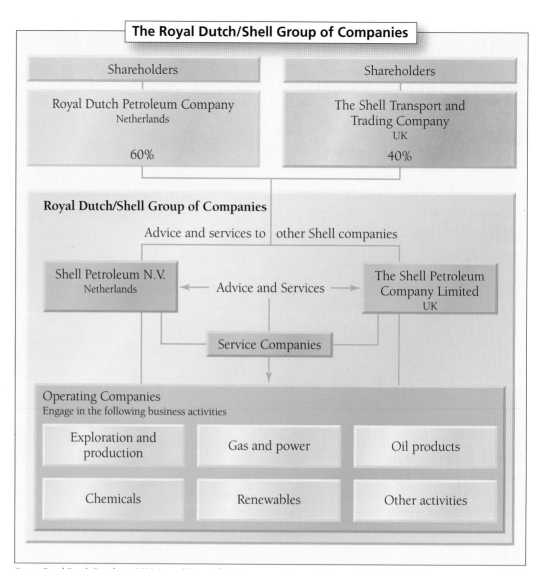

The Royal Dutch/Shell Group of Companies

Shareholders

Royal Dutch Petroleum Company
Netherlands

60%

Shareholders

The Shell Transport and Trading Company
UK

40%

Royal Dutch/Shell Group of Companies

Advice and services to other Shell companies

Shell Petroleum N.V.
Netherlands

← Advice and Services →

The Shell Petroleum Company Limited
UK

Service Companies

Operating Companies
Engage in the following business activities

| Exploration and production | Gas and power | Oil products |
| Chemicals | Renewables | Other activities |

This organizational chart shows the complex relationships among the various Royal Dutch/Shell companies. Royal Dutch Petroleum and the Shell Transport and Trading Company are parent companies of the Royal Dutch/Shell Group, which directly or indirectly holds interests in the service and operating companies.

Source: Royal Dutch Petroleum 2002 Annual Report, http://www.annualreport.shell.com (March 15, 2003).

Combined with the problem of sagging profits, these developments forced Royal Dutch/Shell to reinvent itself. The organization adopted a new policy of publicly reporting its environmental record and actively defending human rights wherever it operated. In 1998 it embarked on a radical restructuring program, slashing costs and personnel and globally reorganizing its various functions, including chemicals, exploration and production, and services. The reorganization marked a significant change from the national-level entities that had previously constituted the Royal Dutch/Shell Group. How this strategy will ultimately play out in the future, as petroleum becomes increasingly scarce and as the burning of fossil fuels causes the Earth to warm, remains to

be seen. Royal Dutch/Shell has demonstrated its ability to plan for and succeed over the long term. It has been able to think globally and act locally as well as any other multinational enterprise in modern history.

Further Reading

Beaton, Kendall. *Enterprise in Oil: A History of Shell in the United States.* New York: Appleton-Century-Crofts, 1957.

Gerretson, Frederick Carel. *History of the Royal Dutch.* 4 vols. Leiden, Netherlands: E. J. Brill, 1953–1957.

Howarth, Stephen. *A Century in Oil: The "Shell" Transport and Trading Company, 1897–1997.* London: Weidenfeld & Nicolson, 1997.

Yergin, Daniel. *The Prize: The Epic Quest for Oil, Money & Power.* New York: Simon & Schuster, 1992.

—*Tyler Priest*

Rule of Law

John Adams declared in 1776 that the United States was "a nation of laws, not men." Ever since, Americans of all political persuasions have invoked the idea of the rule of law as a touchstone for the U.S. system of governance. The rule of law guarantees the individual and corporate rights that are required for a market economy to function and grow. It is the concept within which specific business law topics, for example, contracts and labor law, operate.

What Is the Rule of Law?

The rule of law has three central components. The laws governing a society must be publicly known, understood by the public, and applied equally to all members of a society.

Perhaps the easiest component to grasp is the requirement that laws be public. Laws in the United States today, for example, are readily available to anyone who wishes to see them. Federal and state statutes are published in books and on Web sites and are available in public libraries and from government bookstores. Laws were not always available to the public. Caligula, emperor of Rome, had imperial decrees written in small letters and posted high on pillars so that the decrees could not be read, ensuring that citizens could not know what the law was, much less know whether they had violated it.

Of course laws can be publicly known without a specific member of society having actual knowledge of a particular law, thus the familiar adage that "ignorance of the law is no excuse." Most readers of this encyclopedia will, for example, not know

See also:
Business Law; Constitution, U.S.; Contracts and Contract Law; Private Property.

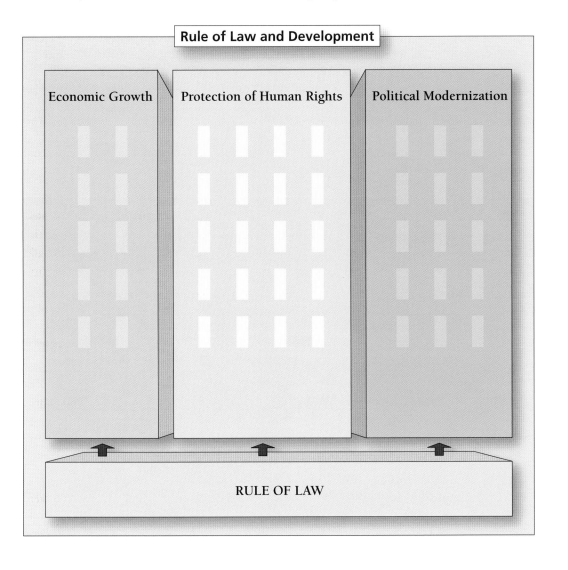

Rule of Law and Development

Economic Growth

Protection of Human Rights

Political Modernization

RULE OF LAW

Some theorists argue that virtually every kind of progress—economic, political, or social—depends on the foundation of the rule of law.

the requirements of the federal Clean Air Act for exhaust gases from automobile engines. Readers could learn those details at any time, however.

The requirement that laws be understandable is potentially more difficult. Laws are often written in technical language and organized according to principles that are not immediately apparent to the average citizen. American lawyers spend three years of postcollege study largely learning how to find the law on any particular topic; lawyers in most other Western countries study for a minimum of five years after high school. Although the use of technical language is not enough to prevent a law from being a legitimate example of the rule of law, at some point the complexity of a particular law may cause it to violate the rule of law by making the law incomprehensible.

The equal application of law is also critical. Equal application requires that no one be exempt from the law's requirements or barred from claiming the benefits of the law. For example, during much of the nineteenth century, England made breaches of employment contracts a criminal offense for employees but not for employers. Thus an employee who quit his job in breach of a contract could be (and often was) prosecuted criminally, but an employer who fired an employee in breach of contract could not be prosecuted.

Equal application also requires that the law be fairly applied by institutions that are competent, fair, and efficient. Courts, police, prosecutors, and defense attorneys must not be corrupt or subject to political manipulation. One means of accomplishing this goal is to make courts independent of political

authorities through autonomy and job security for judges. U.S. federal judges, for example, are appointed effectively for life and cannot have their salaries cut while in office. Thus they are free to rule against the government in citizen suits without fear of retribution.

Finally, equal application requires that the government accept that the law applies to it as well as to the people. Government officials cannot defy courts or refuse to answer lawsuits brought against them by citizens. The power of the U.S. Supreme Court today is a good example of this aspect of the rule of law. The court has a budget that is only a tiny fraction of the federal budget and has no army or significant police force of its own. Yet both Congress and the president readily accede to the Court's rulings, even when doing so undermines their own power.

Business and the Rule of Law

The rule of law is critical to the ability of businesses to function for several reasons. First, the rule of law makes possible the guarantee of individual rights necessary to the functioning of a market economy. In a society governed according to the rule of law, courts will protect individuals' property rights and enforce their contracts, both crucial to a market economy. Second, the rule of law ensures that government rules are fairly and equally applied; where governments can arbitrarily tax businesses, for example, a friend of the president may be able to crush rivals by having their businesses shut down for alleged tax violations. Third, the rule of law allows businesses to plan for the future by ensuring that changes in the legal regulation of business occur openly and with notice.

Where the rule of law is absent, business cannot be transacted. Peruvian economist Hernando de Soto documented the costs of the absence of the rule of law in Peru in the 1980s. His research discovered that "a person of modest means must spend 289 days on bureaucratic procedures to fufill" the legal requirements for setting up a business. The total cost, including lost profits while waiting

---

Importance of Rule of Law to Business

1. Guarantees individual rights necessary for functioning of market economy
2. Protects property rights and enforces contracts critical to market economy
3. Ensures government rules are fairly and equally applied to all businesses
4. Allows businesses to plan for the future

for the bureaucracy to process requests, was over $1,200, more than 32 times the minimum amount necessary to live for a month in Peru at that time.

De Soto concluded that where the rule of law exists, "the confidence created by enforceable contracts makes people more prepared to take risks and these contracts have become requisite for long-term investment. Since innovation is the riskiest investment, if a government cannot give its citizens secure property rights and efficient means of organizing and transferring them—namely contracts—it is denying them one of the main incentives for modernizing and developing their operations." Where the rule of law is absent, business and civil society suffer.

Issues for the Future

Issues concerning the rule of law will continue to arise. New countries, or countries casting off old systems of government, for example, the former Soviet bloc in the 1980s and 1990s, face the difficulty of creating a rule of law where none existed before. As most countries with a tradition of the rule of law developed that tradition gradually and long ago, no obvious body of experience is available to draw upon for creating the rule of law in a short time.

Another important future issue is whether the increasing volume and complexity of laws violates the rule of law. For example, many modern environmental laws are hundreds of pages long. Just as Caligula's decrees violated the rule of law by being unreadable, at some point statutes can become so complex that understanding them is no longer possible for most people.

Finally, many countries have attempted to assist newly independent states, former communist countries, and developing countries to initiate a rule of law. The U.S. government, for example, has funded numerous projects to assist other countries in writing laws and redesigning legal institutions. The ability to translate foreign legal concepts, however, remains an open question for many of these societies. Simply translating

One reason the development community is fostering legal and judicial reform is the belief that, beyond their intrinsic worth, such reforms will help improve economic performance. This belief in the power of legal and judicial reform to spur economic development is supported by a growing body of research showing that economic development is strongly affected by the quality of institutions—including the quality of a nation's legal institutions. . . .

While early work on economic development took for granted the existence of institutions that established clear and enforceable property rights, kept the costs of transacting business to a minimum, and reduced the threat of coercion, more recent work has shown that this is rarely the case. Indeed, current research suggests that the capacity of national institutions to protect property rights, reduce transaction costs, and prevent coercion may be decisive in determining whether economic development takes place.

Furthermore, researchers have started to pay more attention to how institutions that affect the governance of a nation affect economic performance. Government officials respond, at least in part, to the incentives created by political and legal institutions. Therefore, the structure and quality of political institutions can affect whether the government facilitates or inhibits economic development. Stated most simply, the incentives institutions create for government decision-makers will determine whether the government uses its power to create a framework for productive economic activity or to redistribute wealth to itself or its supporters.

—World Bank, "Rule of Law and Development,"
http://www1.worldbank.org/publicsector/legal/ruleoflawanddevelopment.htm
(March 3, 2003)

U.S. laws into the local language is unlikely to be sufficient to establish the rule of law in a country whose immediate past experience is with authoritarian government. How to best assist other countries in developing a rule of law will continue to be a complicated question in the future.

Further Reading

Carothers, Thomas. "The Rule of Law Revival." *Foreign Affairs* 77, no. 2 (April 1998): 95–106.

De Soto, Hernando. *The Other Path: The Invisible Revolution in the Third World*. New York: Harper & Row, 1989.

Dworkin, Ronald. *A Matter of Principle*. Cambridge, Mass.: Harvard University Press, 1985.

Hayek, Friedrich. *The Constitution of Liberty*. Chicago: University of Chicago Press, 1960.

———. *Law, Legislation and Liberty: Rules and Order*. Vol. 1. Chicago: University of Chicago Press, 1973.

Shklar, Judith N. "Political Theory and the Rule of Law." In *The Rule of Law*, edited by A. Hutchinson and P. Monahan. Toronto: Carswell, 1987. Reprinted in Judith N. Shklar, *Political Thought & Political Thinkers*. Chicago: University of Chicago Press, 1998.

—*Andrew P. Morriss*

See also:

Keynes, John Maynard;
Macroeconomics;
Microeconomics.

Samuelson, Paul

1915–
Economist

An academic for nearly 60 years, Paul Samuelson, an economist, lecturer, and author, is known for writing the best-selling economics textbook of all time and for being the first American to receive a Nobel Prize in Economics. He was presented the award in 1970 for improving the analytical methods used in economic theory.

Samuelson was born in 1915 in Gary, Indiana. His father ran a successful drugstore in town. In 1923 the family moved to Chicago, Illinois. In 1932, just shy of turning 17, Samuelson enrolled at the University of Chicago while still in high

Paul Samuelson in Cambridge, Massachusetts, in 1997.

school. Although he enjoyed all of his subjects and toyed with the notion of majoring in sociology, he gravitated toward economics. In the midst of the Great Depression, he forged his beliefs in individualism and the need for social action. He received his bachelor's degree in 1935.

He also received one of eight Social Science Research Council predoctoral fellowships, which were awarded to the eight most-promising economics graduates. He chose to apply his fellowship at Harvard. Samuelson flourished there, leading the march to clarify and systematize economic theory with mathematics. Confronted by contradictions, overlaps, and fallacies in the classical language of economics, Samuelson suggested that mathematics was essential to understanding economics.

As a graduate student, Samuelson wrote many important articles, including "Welfare Economics and International Trade" and "Some Aspects of the Pure Theory of Capital." His article "Interactions between the Multiplier Analysis and the Principle of Acceleration" brought him acclaim from around the world. In the article, he used Keynesian economics (ideas outlined by John Maynard Keynes) to demonstrate the dynamic interactions of consumption, investment, and national income, and to argue that capitalist economic systems were not wildly unstable. At age 22, Samuelson wrote his dissertation, "Foundations of Economic Analysis." When published in book form in 1947, it was an instant success.

Samuelson accepted an instructorship in Harvard's economics department in 1940, but left a month later when offered an assistant professorship at the Massachusetts Institute of Technology (MIT). In 1944 he was appointed associate professor; in 1966 he was named institute professor, the highest professorial rank at the school. Perceived as arrogant toward fellow economists at Chicago and Harvard, Samuelson was also known as a generous teacher. He helped to make MIT's economics department one of the best in the

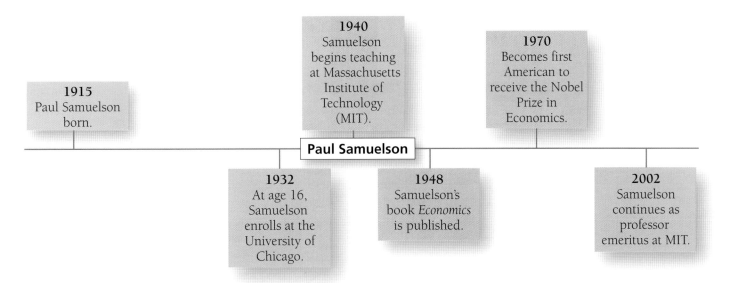

1915
Paul Samuelson born.

1932
At age 16, Samuelson enrolls at the University of Chicago.

1940
Samuelson begins teaching at Massachusetts Institute of Technology (MIT).

1948
Samuelson's book *Economics* is published.

1970
Becomes first American to receive the Nobel Prize in Economics.

Paul Samuelson

2002
Samuelson continues as professor emeritus at MIT.

United States; as of 2002 he continued to serve as professor emeritus.

Economics: An Introductory Analysis, a textbook that he developed from teaching the basic course in economics, was printed in 1948. It was the first textbook to be based on Keynesian principles, and it sent shock waves through the economic world by providing a common economic language for macroeconomic issues including unemployment, inflation, economic growth, and economic equity. It continues to be considered a classic text. Over the last 50 years, *Economics* has sold more than four million copies, has been translated into 41 languages, and has become standard issue for every beginning economics college student in America.

In 1947 the American Economic Association awarded Samuelson the John Bates Clark Medal for the most distinguished contribution to the main body of economic thought and knowledge by a living economist under 40. During his long career, he has explored microeconomics, macroeconomics, welfare economics, and international monetary theory. Samuelson is perhaps best known for his attempt to synthesize neoclassical microeconomics with Keynesian macroeconomics.

Samuelson has also been a magazine columnist, written prolifically for science magazines, and been valued as a consultant by government leaders. He advised Presidents John F. Kennedy and Lyndon B. Johnson and acted as consultant to the U.S. Treasury and the Council of Economic Advisors. He was highly critical of the economic policies of President Richard Nixon and wound up on the administration's notorious enemies list. Throughout his career, Samuelson has tried to apply his mathematical ideas to the service of humanity, working to effect change. The use of logic and function in the search for resolutions is the essence of Samuelson's economic, social, and political philosophies.

Further Reading

Brown, C. Cary, and Robert M. Solow, eds. *Paul Samuelson and Modern Economic Theory.* Boston.: McGraw-Hill, 1983.
Samuelson, Paul, with William Nordhaus. *Economics.* 17th ed. Boston: McGraw-Hill, 2001.
Silk, Leonard. *The Economists.* New York: Basic Books, 1976.

—*Sheri Rehwoldt*

I came into economics at a fortunate time—when the world was misbehaving in depression and inflation and just when academic opportunity was exploding at more than exponential rates. At Chicago, Harvard, and MIT, precisely when and where the action was heating up, I was there. The tide raises all ships, and once among the leaders, I had only to sail as fast as the fleet to retain lead position. Best of all have been the hundreds of companions at arms acquired along the way.

—Paul Samuelson, *Journal of Economic Education*, 1999

Santa Fe Trail

See also:
Hudson's Bay Company;
Transportation Industry.

The Santa Fe Trail is a historic route over which trade goods were transported between Santa Fe (in present-day New Mexico) and the eastern United States between 1821 and 1880. The trail was never a road in the modern sense, but rather a general route followed by traders and their wagons. In what is today western Kansas, the trail split. The mountain route traversed southern Colorado, crossing over Raton Pass into New Mexico, while the Cimarron Cutoff went south, crossing what is today the Oklahoma Panhandle. The Santa Fe Trail is important to the history of U.S. business because it played a key role in connecting the eastern part of the country with the western territories, to which the trail was an economic lifeline.

Interest in establishing trade between New Mexico and the Missouri country dated to the 1700s, when New Mexico was the northernmost colony of the Spanish Empire in the Americas. Trade goods that New Mexicans needed were brought north from Mexico on the Camino Real (Royal Road). The prices the colonists paid were high and the goods were of low quality. Spain, however, did not allow New Mexicans

Santa Fe Trail

1821
William Becknell is first to follow the route later known as the Santa Fe Trail.

1825
United States signs treaty with the Osage tribe for a public highway called the Santa Fe Trail.

1832
Independence, Missouri, becomes the eastern outfitting point for the trail.

1849 to 1852
California Gold Rush increases westbound travel over the trail.

1860s
Santa Fe Trail shortened as the railroads push west.

1880
The railroad reaches Santa Fe, ending the Santa Fe Trail as a major transportation route.

The Santa Fe Trail

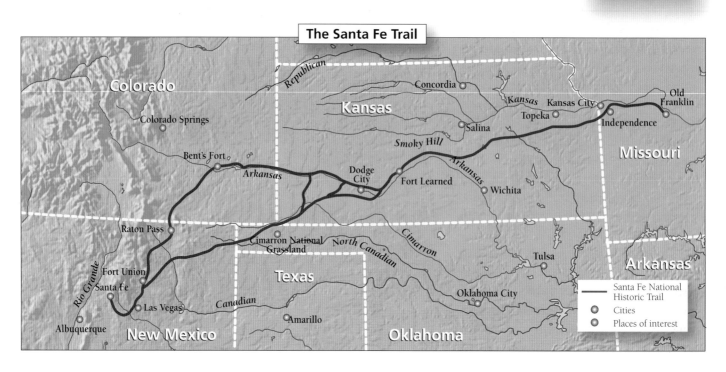

Santa Fe National Historic Trail
○ Cities
○ Places of interest

to trade with non-Spanish suppliers except with government permission, which was rarely granted. An example of the difficulties facing traders is the case of Pierre and Paul Mallet of St. Louis (then a French settlement), who initially received permission to bring goods into New Mexico. However, when they arrived in Santa Fe in 1749, they were arrested and sent to Mexico City, where they were imprisoned and never heard of again. Nevertheless, French traders and, after the Missouri country passed to the United States through the Louisiana Purchase, Americans continued to attempt trading expeditions to Santa Fe.

William Becknell, known as the "father of the Santa Fe Trail," led the first truly successful expedition from the east to Santa Fe in 1821. Becknell heard that Mexico had revolted against Spanish rule and assumed that Spanish restrictions on trade would be removed. He advertised in a Missouri newspaper for men to go west to trade horses and mules. He did not refer to carrying trade goods or name Santa Fe as his destination because he did not want to

attract the attention of Spanish authorities if the revolution had been a failure. When the Becknell party left Franklin, Missouri, on September 1, it included a number of packhorses loaded with merchandise.

Becknell's party followed the Arkansas River across the Great Plains and came through the mountains of present-day Colorado. The Mexican Revolution had

A lithograph entitled The Santa Fe Trail in the Fra Cristobal Mountains, *circa 1845.*

An undated political cartoon shows speculators selling land in Oklahoma for $2.

succeeded, and the traders were welcomed in Santa Fe and made excellent profits. In 1822 Becknell led a second expedition to Santa Fe. This time the company took three wagons loaded with merchandise and followed a more level route from western Kansas into New Mexico; a passage became known as the Cimarron Cutoff. No water was available along this route, however, and the Becknell party nearly died of thirst before killing a buffalo and drinking the water in its stomach.

At first, the trail started in Franklin, but as population shifted westward, traders were able to purchase merchandise farther west, and the eastern terminus shifted to Independence, Missouri, and then to eastern Kansas. During the Civil War, the Union Pacific Railway began laying track westward in Kansas, and as the track progressed toward Santa Fe, the eastern terminus also moved west as traders could ship goods more cheaply by rail than by wagon.

Trade on the Santa Fe Trail grew almost every year. Soon more goods were traveling to Santa Fe than could be sold there. Traders began to go south into Mexico on the Camino Real to the larger markets of Chihuahua and Durango. By the end of the 1830s, many New Mexican merchants were participating in the Santa Fe trade, traveling east to buy American goods for their stores or to be shipped south to Mexico or west to California. New Mexicans also exported goods east. Mules from New Mexico were especially prized by Americans.

Indian attacks were a major impediment to Santa Fe trade. Kiowa, Comanche, Pawnee, and many other tribes hunted in the land crossed by the trail. For safety, traders formed wagon caravans, but even these were often attacked. In 1833 Congress established a regiment to guard caravans on the Santa Fe Trail.

In 1846 war broke out between Mexico and the United States when the U.S. annexed the Republic of Texas, a former Mexican possession. U.S. general Stephen Watts Kearny led an army west on the Santa Fe Trail. Entering Santa Fe without opposition, he claimed New Mexico as a United States territory and declared the people of New Mexico American citizens. Traffic on the trail increased because traders no longer had to pay tariffs on their merchandise and because the American army was a new market for their goods. To establish a U.S.

Mrs. Mary Burleson of Carrizozo, New Mexico, was 78 years old when she gave this interview to a representative of the Federal Writers Project in 1938.

Pioneer Recollections

Our family left West Port, Missouri, which is Kansas City, Missouri, now, in April 1865, and arrived in Mora, New Mexico, in September 1865. We came over the Santa Fe Trail in a prairie schooner drawn by six oxen and our milk cow, for this was the only way we had of bringing our milk cow with us. We were in a government train guarded by soldiers, as the Indians were on the warpath at that time and were always on the look out for settlers that were moving out to the west. . . .

We saw many large herds of buffalo on our trip. It rained a lot that summer and we had no hardships as to feed and water. It took us from April to September. I remember the great event in our home was the arrival of the *St. Louis Globe Democrat* and when it came all the neighbors would come to our house and my father would read the paper to them by candlelight. We made all our own candles in those days. Sometimes it happened that we would not get the paper on time and then we would hear that the Indians had held up a stage coach and burned the mail. How we would miss the paper. My father took this same paper for 50 years. There were no schools much in those days. Sometimes a teacher was hired by private subscription and all the children in a neighborhood would go to school and often the children would know as much as the teacher.

—Mrs. Mary Burleson, 1938

An adobe wall of Fort Union at what is now Fort Union National Monument in New Mexico. Three successive U.S. Army forts, which were used to defend the Santa Fe Trail, occupied this site.

presence and to house the soldiers who protected traders from Indian raids, Fort Union was built in 1851 at the point where the mountain and Cimarron branches of the trail rejoined. Other forts were later established along the trail, and supplying them became an important industry.

Trade continued to increase along the Santa Fe Trail through the Civil War, but the trail grew shorter and shorter after the war as the railroad moved west. When the railroad reached Santa Fe in 1880, the trail ceased to exist as a trading route. The trail began to disappear as weeds grew over the deep tracks made by traders' wagons over several decades. However, in 1902 the Kansas chapter of the Daughters of the American Revolution initiated a movement to map the trail and to put up markers along the route. Contemporary travelers can follow the trail that created a commercial bond between New Mexico and the United States.

Further Reading

Dart, David. *The Santa Fe Trail.* New York: Alfred A. Knopf, 2001.

Peters, Arthur King. *Seven Trails West.* New York: Abbeville Press, 1996.

Simmons, Marc. *Following the Santa Fe Trail: A Guide for Modern Travelers.* 2nd ed. Santa Fe, N.M.: Ancient City Press, 1986.

—*Jean Caldwell*

See also:
Arts and Entertainment
Industry; Telecommunications
Industry.

Sarnoff, David

1891–1971
Television pioneer

Starting life in the United States as a poor immigrant, David Sarnoff made himself into a successful and powerful business leader. He played a key role in creating America's radio and television broadcast industry.

Sarnoff was born in Russia near the city of Minsk in 1891 to Abraham and Leah Sarnoff. Abraham was a painter and the family had little money. In 1896 Abraham moved to the United States, hoping to earn enough money to enable his family to join him. While Abraham was away, young Sarnoff studied to become a rabbi and a Talmudic scholar.

When Sarnoff arrived in Manhattan in 1900, he found his father seriously ill. At age nine Sarnoff set to work to help support his family. He earned money by singing at his synagogue, and he sold Yiddish newspapers every afternoon. He opened his own newspaper stand at age 13 and employed his brothers to help him run it. He also studied English, both in school and by reading newspapers. At age 15 he graduated from elementary school.

Sarnoff needed more money than he could earn by operating a newsstand, however, and

An undated photograph shows a young David Sarnoff working as a telegraph operator.

he decided to apply for a job at the *New York Herald* newspaper. In searching for the *Herald*, he made a wrong turn and found himself in the offices of the Commercial Cable Company. The wrong turn changed Sarnoff's life. The Commercial Cable Company hired Sarnoff as a messenger boy and fired him not long after when he objected to his boss's decision not to give him time off for observance of the Jewish holidays Rosh Hashanah and Yom Kippur. He worked at the cable company long enough, however, to learn to operate a telegraph key—a skill that would prove to be valuable to him in his next job at the American Marconi Wireless Telegraph Company. He worked first as an office boy at American Marconi, preparing himself for promotion by reading company documents he was assigned to file. He also read technical journals and observed the work of Marconi's engineers. Soon after his sixteenth birthday Sarnoff was promoted to the position of junior wireless operator, at a salary of $7.50 per week.

Sarnoff's career soared after the famous sinking of the *Titanic* in 1912. A popular version of the story says the young wireless operator was the first to hear of the accident, but historians report that he was not at work on the night of the sinking. When he did learn of the sinking, however, Sarnoff worked for 72 hours straight, obtaining information from friends and relatives of *Titanic* survivors and victims and conveying the information to others by wireless messages. His actions impressed the Marconi managers and earned him a promotion.

In 1916 Sarnoff submitted an idea for "radio music boxes" to E. J. Nally, vice president of American Marconi. Sarnoff, who was only 25 years old at the time, suggested that music, news, sports, and lectures could be made available to listeners by a system not very different from the radio system then in use by navigators in the shipping industry. Nally rejected the idea, but Sarnoff proposed it again in 1920 when the Radio Corporation of America (RCA), controlled by General Electric (GE), absorbed Marconi. GE agreed to provide $2,000 for the development of a prototype radio music box; commercial

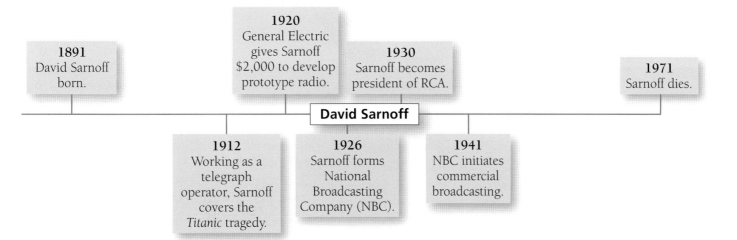

1891
David Sarnoff born.

1920
General Electric gives Sarnoff $2,000 to develop prototype radio.

1930
Sarnoff becomes president of RCA.

1971
Sarnoff dies.

David Sarnoff

1912
Working as a telegraph operator, Sarnoff covers the *Titanic* tragedy.

1926
Sarnoff forms National Broadcasting Company (NBC).

1941
NBC initiates commercial broadcasting.

radio was born that year on several amateur stations, including KDKA in Pittsburgh, the country's first licensed radio station.

Not until 1921, however, did Sarnoff realize much success with his new idea. On July 2, 1921, Sarnoff, then the general manager of RCA, captured a large radio audience when he arranged to broadcast a heavyweight boxing match between Jack Dempsey and Georges Carpentier. With the success of this broadcast, Americans were hooked in large numbers on listening to the radio. Within three years RCA earned more than $80 million in revenue from radio sales.

In 1923 as the U.S. government explored early allegations that RCA, Westinghouse, AT&T, and GE had conspired illegally to restrain trade in the broadcast industry, Sarnoff proposed a restructuring of RCA. He envisioned new opportunities, including the creation of broadcast networks—national broadcasts linked to one another at hundreds of radio stations—and in 1926 he formed the National Broadcasting Company (NBC). From network radio broadcasting he turned to television, launching an experimental NBC television station in 1928. In 1939 he demonstrated television technology at the New York World's Fair. In 1941 NBC initiated commercial telecasting, but it did not attract large audiences until after World War II.

As Sarnoff's stature grew in the broadcasting industry, the U.S. government took notice, calling upon him in 1929 to assist with negotiations for a war reparations treaty with Germany. Sarnoff also served the war effort during World War II, directing press operations associated with the Allied invasion of France (June 1944), for which he was awarded the rank of brigadier general and the Legion of Merit.

The government continued to pursue legal action against RCA, however. After Sarnoff became president of RCA in 1930, he spent two years trying to convince federal officials not to break up an RCA patent-sharing arrangement about which other companies had complained, alleging unfair competition. The breakup would damage a communications industry suffering from effects of the Great Depression, Sarnoff argued, and it might encourage foreign companies to attempt to gain control of the American market for radio broadcasting. In a 1932 compromise settlement, RCA, Westinghouse, and GE were split apart from one another, and Sarnoff maintained sole leadership of RCA.

Sarnoff was a strong leader and an aggressive competitor. In 1933 Edwin Armstrong of RCA developed a new radio broadcast system called frequency modulation (known as FM today). At the time, FM produced significantly less static than Sarnoff's AM system, and it carried sound better. When Sarnoff rejected FM, Armstrong left the company to pursue the FM idea on his own; he also sued RCA and NBC, claiming that they had attempted to hinder his efforts. Sarnoff and Armstrong had been friends prior to this dispute, but Sarnoff's

A still image from the first television broadcast, at the 1939 World's Fair: David Sarnoff at the dedication ceremony for the RCA Building.

request; at the same time he issued hasty orders directing RCA engineers to develop color-compatible RCA television sets. The FCC finally approved the CBS request in 1950, only to reverse its decision in 1953. Sarnoff had assumed the role of chairman of the board at RCA in 1947. Under his leadership, NBC produced the first made-for-television movie.

During the cold war decades of the 1950s and 1960s, Sarnoff frequently spoke out against communism. He served as an aide to Vice President Richard Nixon on an anticommunism media campaign. He proposed dropping radios in communist countries to send messages about democracy during the height of that tense time. He supported Senator Joseph McCarthy's hunts for communists in the United States (in what became known as the Red Scare), and he blocked certain individuals from working for RCA for political reasons.

Sarnoff worked to develop basic computer technology within RCA during the 1970s. He retired at the age of 79 in 1970 and died a year later. In 1986 RCA was taken over by GE, the company from which it was separated in 1932.

Sarnoff's name lives on in the Sarnoff Corporation, based in West Windsor, New Jersey. The Sarnoff Corporation specializes in information, biomedical, and electronic technologies. The multimillion-dollar company was founded by RCA Laboratories in 1942 and named after Sarnoff in 1951. In 1987 it became a subsidiary of SRI International.

Sarnoff was a shrewd businessman and a pioneer in the development of broadcast media technology. His ideas and efforts brought radio and television broadcasting into American homes and shaped the American communications industry throughout the twentieth century.

lawyers battled Armstrong in court for six years, and Armstrong committed suicide in 1954. Philo Farnsworth, the first inventor to patent an electronic television system, also sued RCA, claiming that RCA engineer Vladmir Zworykin had applied for a patent based on information he gathered from a visit to Farnsworth's laboratory. The courts eventually agreed with Farnsworth, but his patent elapsed before he could make much money from his invention.

Sarnoff also took quick action in 1945 to stem the early development of color television. CBS had requested Federal Communication Commission (FCC) approval for color television broadcasting. RCA television sets could receive only black-and-white programming. Anyone with an RCA television would have to buy a new one to receive color broadcasting from CBS. Sarnoff saw this prospect as a threat that could destroy RCA. In response he lobbied the FCC in opposition to the CBS

Further Reading

Bilby, Kenneth. *The General: David Sarnoff and the Rise of the Communications Industry*. New York: Harper Trade, 1986.

Lyons, Eugene. *David Sarnoff: A Biography*. New York: Harper & Row, 1966.

—Karen Ayres

Glossary

communism Economic and social system based on group ownership of the means of production; goods and services are allocated by the central government. See encyclopedia entry.

cost–benefit analysis Evaluating the monetary and nonmonetary gains and losses that ensue from making various choices. See encyclopedia entry, Cost.

credit union Nonprofit financial institution owned by its members that functions as a bank.

deregulation Process of removing government restrictions on business.

direct investment Investment in businesses located in other countries. See encyclopedia entry, Globalization.

economies of scale Declining average cost of production that results from increasing output. See encyclopedia entry.

encryption Encoding information.

entrepreneur Person who combines different resources to make goods or services available to others. See encyclopedia entry, Entrepreneurship.

fiscal policy Process of managing economic expansions and contractions by adjusting government spending to stabilize incomes and economic performance. See encyclopedia entry.

franchise License to operate a business that is part of a larger chain. See encyclopedia entry.

insurance Financial protection against loss. See encyclopedia entry, Insurance Industry.

intellectual property Creations of the mind, for example, literary works and graphic designs. See encyclopedia entry.

inventory The supply of goods held by a business. See encyclopedia entry.

joint venture Two or more businesses cooperating to produce a good or service.

Keynesian principles Theories of economist John Maynard Keynes; the idea that governments can positively influence the business cycle through spending and taxation policies. See encyclopedia entry, Keynes, John Maynard.

license A kind of contract that grants permission to manufacture, copy, distribute, sell, or use intellectual property, for example, inventions and patents; or, government approval to take an action or engage in an activity. See encyclopedia entry.

litigation Process of bringing a lawsuit.

macroeconomics Study of an economy as a whole. See encyclopedia entry.

market capitalization Total value of a corporation's outstanding shares.

market economy Economic system wherein decisions are made in markets and based on the forces of supply and demand.

market segmentation Marketing method that focuses on groups of consumers that share specific characteristics, for example, age, sex, or income.

market share Percentage of all dollars spent on a product or service that a specific company earns for that product or service; the proportion of a particular market dominated by a specific company.

mass media Any message produced by a small group intended for consumption by a large group; commercials are a form of mass media. See encyclopedia entry, Advertising Industry.

microeconomics Study of the decisions made by individuals and firms. See encyclopedia entry.

monetary policy Government's use of its power over the money supply to influence economic growth and inflation. See encyclopedia entry.

monopoly Type of market that involves only one seller. See encyclopedia entry.

natural monopoly Situation in which competition does not result in cheaper goods or services; rather one firm is able to provide a good or service at lowest cost to consumers. See encyclopedia entry, Monopoly.

oligopoly Market dominated by a few sellers.

public goods Goods that everyone can enjoy equally and no one can be excluded from; fresh air and national defense are public goods. See encyclopedia entry.

public utility Range of industries owned by the state that provide services like transportation, communication, gas, power, and water.

real estate investment trust (REIT) Investment vehicles, similar to mutual funds, that allow small investors to invest in real estate. See encyclopedia entries, Investment; Mutual Funds.

securities Stocks, bonds, and other financial instruments. See encyclopedia entry, Stocks and Bonds.

strategic alliance Two or more businesses working together to produce a good or service or increase profits by seeking greater efficiencies; some companies form strategic alliances to reduce costs by ordering in bulk.

subsidy Government financial support of a business endeavor. See encyclopedia entry.

trust Business structure that mandates all decisions in an industry be made by a central body for all producers in an attempt to raise prices and profitability. See encyclopedia entry, Monopoly.

warranty Guarantee by the producer or seller of a product to make certain repairs within a set amount of time.

Index

Page numbers in **boldface** type indicate article titles. Page numbers in *italic* type indicate illustrations or other graphics.